PRAISE FOR
Zamba

"Wonderful, detailed . . . amusing. . . . *Zamba* is a charming read."
—*People* magazine

"Legendary Hollywood animal trainer and behaviorist Ralph Helfer captures an incredible story of love between man and lion that displays all the qualities that made his previous book, *Modoc: The True Story of the Greatest Elephant That Ever Lived*, so moving. . . . Will touch the heart of any animal lover."
—*Publishers Weekly*

"Extraordinary. . . . Beautifully expresses a simple philosophy so many have trouble following: respect for all living creatures, given and returned."
—*Kirkus Reviews*

"A warmhearted tale of love between two species."
—*Booklist*

"A fascinating book. . . . Humorous and touching."
—*School Library Journal*

About the Author

RALPH HELFER is a well-known Hollywood animal behaviorist who was one of the first to use affection and kindness to train wild animals. He is a producer, director, and lecturer as well as the author of *Mosey, The Beauty of the Beasts,* and *Modoc.* He lives in Newport Beach and in Kenya, where he leads safari tours.

ZAMBA

ZAMBA

The True Story of
the Greatest Lion
That Ever Lived

RALPH HELFER

HARPER

NEW YORK · LONDON · TORONTO · SYDNEY

HARPER

A hardcover edition of this book was published in 2005 by HarperCollins Publishers.

ZAMBA. Copyright © 2005 by Ralph Helfer. All rights reserved. Printed in the United States of America. No part of this book may be used or reproduced in any manner whatsoever without written permission except in the case of brief quotations embodied in critical articles and reviews. For information address HarperCollins Publishers, 10 East 53rd Street, New York, NY 10022.

HarperCollins books may be purchased for educational, business, or sales promotional use. For information please write: Special Markets Department, HarperCollins Publishers, 10 East 53rd Street, New York, NY 10022.

First Harper paperback published 2006.

Designed by Jaime Putorti
All photographs courtesy of Ralph Helfer

The Library of Congress has catalogued the hardcover edition as follows:
Helfer, Ralph.
    Zamba : the true story of the greatest lion that ever lived / by Ralph Helfer.—1st ed.
      p. cm.
    ISBN 0-06-076132-6
    1. Zamba (Lion). 2. Lions—California—Los Angeles—Biography. 3. Animals in motion pictures—California—Los Angeles—Biography. 4. Helfer, Ralph. 5. Animal trainers—California—Los Angeles—Biography. I. Title.

Sf408.6.L54H45 2005
599.757'092'9—dc22   2004054341

ISBN-10: 0-06-076133-4 (pbk.)
ISBN-13: 978-0-06-076133-2 (pbk.)

06 07 08 09 10 ❖/RRD 10 9 8 7 6 5 4 3 2 1

Dedicated
to
Mom, Dad, and my sister Sally Ann

Acknowledgments

I wish to thank Rebecca St. John, my West Coast editor, for having the tenacity to stick with me through the early stages of the book. She understands the way I look at nature and its animals. Her feelings for animals parallel mine, and she provided the guidance necessary to put the book on the right path.

To Laura Tucker, my newfound East Coast friend and editor, who permeated the book with new thinking and direction. Her ability to understand my emotional feelings toward animals allowed her to create a continuity that kept the book on the right track, and melded it into a fluid read.

For the final edit HarperCollins publishers graciously allowed Kelly Bare to take my four years of writing and put everything together to create the final book. One would have thought her an animal behaviorist, the way she swept through the many pages of animal lore and put them in the correct perspective.

Jill Schwartzman picked up the baton and took us to the finish line with patience and good grace.

My heartfelt thanks to HarperCollins for their faith in me through two books—*Modoc* and now *Zamba*.

My gratitude and affection to my agent, Richard Curtis, for his support and belief in me on a most unusual project. Through his guidance the book has kept its impact and stayed on course.

I also wish to thank my many African friends who came to my rescue and assisted me in remembering anecdotes and incidents that occurred in East Africa.

My days with Zamba were shared by two very loving and special people: Toni and my daughter, Tana. They were there during most of the time Zamba was in my life. They loved him as I did. We were "family." And together we shared both the happy and the sad moments that came our way. I couldn't have done it without them.

To Suzzi, my Loving African Princess, who was there whether in the middle of the night or sitting in the hot Serengeti veldt helping me through the volumes of paperwork that eventually would become *Zamba*. It was her essence of sharing my world that made it all possible.

To Cathi, my sister, whose love and devotion has seen me through the many years of struggle. Her belief in me and my unusual world of nature and its animals has helped me climb the ladder of achievement. She has always been there for me.

 **Preface**

The writing of *Zamba* has been both an emotional and a reward-
ing experience. It allowed me to relive eighteen years of my life
with a true and loyal friend.

Living with an African lion, bringing him into my world and
teaching him to be patient and understanding with us humans,
was an in-depth study of the potential of human-animal relationships. But what was more important was how Zamba taught me
his way of life and allowed me to enter into his domain and share
the unique God-given wonders offered to him.

I realize now more than ever before that animals are indeed perfect. As a result of living by nature's law, they live a life as God in-
tended. We humans, unlike animals, have the power of choice and
therefore have the ability to go against nature and do whatever we
desire. Unfortunately our choices are not always the right ones.

Writing about living with a lion brought back all the grand moments we shared. As I wrote, I felt as if each event was actually
happening one more time, and I trembled with excitement, just as

before. I smiled, even laughed aloud when I remembered a cherished occasion. But there were hard times, too, and when I recalled the tender moments, my tears flowed, and I had to close the book until the sadness was not too much to bear.

Now, please settle back, open your hearts, and share my life with Zamba, the greatest lion that ever lived.

ZAMBA

I have spent my life living and working peacefully with animals. But one of my most formative learning experiences was an incident that ended with me in the hospital.

I was in my late teens. I was doing stunts and assisting other trainers with their animals, and I was offered a job as a stuntman for a Hollywood studio. They asked that I work an adult male lion on a pedestal, just as is done in the circus. They wanted him to snarl and swipe at me a few times.

I told them I'd be happy to, but for one problem: I had no lion. I said thanks anyhow and hung up.

Later that day the studio called again. They said that they'd found a lion. The man who owned him would be out of town for the day of the shoot, but he knew of me and felt I could do the stunt. He said that the lion, who was called Rex, was old and would respond to certain basic commands. The handler who'd be bringing Rex to the shoot could tell me everything I needed to know.

I could hardly contain my excitement. I had been obsessed with lions since childhood, and I held them in the highest esteem, more than any other creature. To me they represented the best that nature had to offer. Their regal attitude, proud stance, strength, and dignity always made me feel I was in the presence of royalty, and I felt a real spiritual connection to them—I felt called to work with them.

I have always been convinced that very real communication between humans and animals is possible, and I was sure that working with a lion was my own key to that interaction. But at that time in my career I hadn't yet set foot in an arena with any animal, let alone with a lion. And this job wasn't the way I had imagined my first solo interaction with a lion would be. I knew that this animal had been "fear trained," and working with an animal that had been tamed with cruelty and violence went against all my principles. I also realized that it had the potential to be very, very dangerous.

In spite of my reservations, the studio made it hard to refuse the job. They said I was just the right size, and they offered me a good deal of money. Times were rough. I had acquired a number of small animals—raccoons, opossums, kinkajous, a red-tailed hawk, and a small mountain lion—and my expenses had escalated. I reasoned with my conscience: after all, I hadn't had anything to do with the lion's training, and I certainly wouldn't be hurting him. In fact, it could be the other way around. I accepted.

The hard part was telling my girlfriend.

"Ralph, you're an idiot! This is an incredibly stupid thing to do. You don't know the lion, and he's never met you. You can't get instructions from some guy five minutes before you go into the ring to work a lion."

"The trainer said it won't be a problem, and I really need the money."

"We don't need it that badly. You're going to get yourself killed."

Sweet, athletic Laura had helped me build my small collection of animals. We argued for hours, until she finally gave up on me.

"Go ahead—kill yourself. Enjoy your short career."

In my heart, I knew she was right. But I needed the money, and I wanted to prove to myself that I could do it. Although I didn't agree with the methods of trainers who used fear, I had seen what they did and how they did it, and I felt I could mimic their commands. I didn't need to abuse the animal—I was just going to be following the directions I was given, issuing commands that the owner had trained the lion to respond to years before. The handler who accompanied the lion would tell me what to do and how to do it, and I'd be home by lunch.

On the day of the shoot, when I arrived at the studio I noticed a pickup truck and trailer parked near the entrance to the big soundstage. Actually, it wasn't the pickup I noticed so much as the enormous African lion pacing in a large portable cage nearby, jaws dripping with saliva. A man dressed in a pair of well-worn jeans, a striped Western shirt, cowboy boots, and a broad-brimmed hat stood near the cage. The telltale string coming out of his shirt pocket meant he was carrying a small bag of "Bullderm" chewing tobacco.

I introduced myself and asked how the lion was feeling. The handler cocked his hat back on his balding head and said, "Well, okay, I guess."

"You guess?" I questioned.

"Well, yeah, a bit restless, but . . ." He hesitated. "He's okay."

A squirt of tobacco juice landed on the ground near me. "When do these people pay us?" he asked.

I'd seen this type of guy hanging around the barns at some of the animal compounds. He was a mess of uncouth habits and flaunted his couldn't-care-less attitude.

"I think they'll pay by check in about a week," I said.

Another stream of spit hit the dirt.

I saw the situation for what it was. This fellow needed money, and he'd let me work the lion—even if it was unsafe—just to get it. I felt a strange sensation in my stomach. But I didn't back out. In the next two minutes he told me all that he knew about Rex, which was how to get him to sit on the pedestal, cuff at me with his paw, and snarl.

"That's it," he said.

"That's it?"

"That's it—no big deal."

"Has he ever been handled?"

"You mean touched?"

I nodded yes.

"Are you crazy? He'd kill you!"

My opinion of this guy sank even lower—and my nerves weren't improving.

"Okay, kid, we're ready for you." A man spoke from the slightly open door of the soundstage.

There were about thirty-five people on the set. Assistant directors, set decorators, electricians, carpenters, script girl—it's always amazing to me how many people it takes behind the camera to make a movie.

The director, the person responsible for what happens in front of the camera, came over and introduced himself. He cautioned me not to turn around; I was doubling an actor who was my size and build, and he needed my back to the camera.

"Get the lion in up on the pedestal and make him snarl and cuff at you with his paw. If you can do that, we'll have our print and we can all go home. Okay?" he asked.

"Okay," I answered, more confidently than I felt.

I was escorted to makeup and wardrobe, and for the next hour I was made up to look like the actor. I was dressed in a standard blue and gold arena costume, with high boots, gold epaulets dangling on my shoulders, and a proper beaked cap on my head.

Back on the set, I saw they had set up a steel arena on the stage, with a circus scene backdrop. The cement floor in the arena was covered with a thick layer of sawdust. In the middle stood a heavy metal pedestal. A line of portable cages had been rolled up and positioned to form a chute, leading to a side door in the arena. Rex had settled down and was lying complacently at the far end of the chute. The director showed me my mark—the spot where I was to stand. It seemed a bit close to Rex's pedestal, but I was not in any state of mind to question it.

I took my mark.

"Roll camera!" yelled the assistant director.

Cameras rolled.

"Action!" yelled the director.

I held the whip and the chair that Rex's handler had brought. A pistol was strapped to my belt, but I hadn't checked to see whether it was real or not. I nervously nodded for the handler to open the chute door and cracked the whip to signal the lion in, per the instructions I'd been given. The handler took a long pole and jabbed Rex in the belly. The lion responded by roaring in anger, jumping to his feet, and charging into the ring. He was huge, with a full mane, and I figured he had to weigh a good five hundred pounds.

I breathed for what felt like the first time in days. Well, I thought, he's in the ring. That's one down—two tricks to go.

He mounted the pedestal without me giving any cues at all. That was two. I jockeyed into position to get the snarl and cuff. I cracked the whip and gave the cue the handler had given me, and Rex gave a full snarl and his best MGM roar, lashing out at me with his massive paw. That's three, I thought. It's over. I heard the director yell, "Cut."

I've never felt so relieved in my life. My costume was soaked in sweat, but the scene had gone beautifully. I backed away and was about to give the signal to raise the chute door when I heard the director say, "That was great, son. Let's do it again."

What? How could we do better than that first take? In the years to come, I was to learn that directors *always* want that second shot.

"Tight shot on the lion!" he yelled. The cameramen fussed with their equipment. I tried my best to keep Rex on the pedestal until they were ready, but I could tell he was getting nervous.

After a few minutes the assistant director yelled again, "Roll camera!"

"Action!" yelled the director.

My sweat-soaked costume was beginning to chafe. The arm holding the chair was shaking, and the whip felt as if it weighed fifty pounds. In a near panic I approached the lion. Again I gave the cue, and again he snarled. But this time I thought I glimpsed a different look in his eyes, as though he was realizing for the first time that I wasn't his real trainer. As I stepped into position to be cuffed, I saw his hind end move from a sitting position to a crouch. His ears disappeared into his mane, and a low, guttural, vibrato growl came from his throat. His huge eyes changed from tawny to blood red.

Oh shit! I thought.

Rex launched himself at me. The force of his lunge shot the pedestal back a full fifteen feet, and it hit the steel bars with a deafening clang. His front feet hit the ground only once before he reached me. He nailed me full in the chest, knocking me to the ground. The force was astonishing, and my head struck hard against the cement floor hiding under the sawdust. I saw a whirl of fur, flaming eyes, flashing teeth. The stench of his rancid breath filled my lungs.

All of a sudden, my arm was in his mouth. I actually heard my flesh pop as he sank his fang into my wrist. I put my arm over my face for protection and saw a huge, gaping hole where he'd punctured my wrist. Blood poured out onto my face and chest. I felt his hind claws ripping at my legs through the costume.

I looked up, and what I saw still gives me night sweats to this day. Rex was on top of me, his face not more than a foot from mine. He was roaring in defiance and rage, with blood—my blood!—soaking the fur around his mouth and dripping from his fangs. His crimson eyes were full of hatred.

Shock overcame me as I realized I was about to be killed. Strangely, the emotion I felt most strongly wasn't fear or pain, but anger. I was pissed. Obviously I had done something wrong. What? I didn't know. But I was furious at myself. I loved animals, and I knew that I could help them to communicate effectively with humans, so that we could work and live together in peaceful harmony. What was I doing here?

People were running around outside the arena screaming, but no one was coming in to help.

Blood from my wrist clouded my eyes, and I couldn't see. I was afraid to move, to resist in any way. Then I heard the steel arena door squeak open. Someone was coming! Someone was dragging something heavy across the cement floor, and suddenly there was a deafening, high-pitched noise, like a truck tire exploding. I strained to see what was happening, but all I could see was a dense cloud of smokelike vapor filling the arena. Using me as a launching platform, Rex leaped for the chute door. I knew he was safely enclosed when I heard the door slam shut.

I felt a number of hands pick me up and carry me outside, from the arena, through the lot, onto the street. Someone with a wet cloth wiped the blood from my face. I shaded my face from the sun and noticed sunlight shining through the hole where Rex's fang had gone through my wrist.

"We can't wait for the ambulance!" someone shouted. "Load him in here!"

I had a blurred view of a station wagon and someone lowering the back gate. "Where are you going with my new station wagon?" a woman yelled.

"This man needs to be taken to a hospital, now!"

Apparently her car was the only one parked in front of the stage door with the keys in the ignition.

"Don't let him bleed on my upholstery!" I heard her say. It was the last thing I heard for a while.

I woke up in the hospital, feeling as if I'd been run over by a freight train. I was bandaged all up and down my legs and arms. Rex's claws had ripped skin from all over my body, and he'd broken a few ribs when he used me as his launchpad. The worst part was the bite on my wrist.

"It went clean through," said the doctor. "Quarter inch either way and he would have severed an artery. You could have lost your hand."

When my visitors had left and I was alone for the night, I lay in that hospital bed and thought about what had happened—why the scene had gone the way it had. The attack did more than physically hurt me; it woke me up. My love of lions had blinded me to the dangers they posed. Of course, I'd known in some abstract way that lions were dangerous, but I had never dreamed that one would turn on me.

Rex had been my first close encounter with a large exotic, and while it wasn't exactly what I'd had in mind, when I think about it now, it was probably the best thing that could have happened.

Animals aren't toys, or robots. Laura had been right; you can't get instructions on handling a lion five minutes before you enter a ring with him. You need to have a *relationship* with an animal before you can work together, and that doesn't go just for lions or other animals that can do you harm, but for *all* animals. There must be a tremendous amount of respect and trust between an animal and a human working together, or both of them are at terrific risk.

The worst part was that I'd known this, but my greed and my passion had gotten in the way. As a result, I'd come very close to losing my hand, and maybe even my life.

After I was released from the hospital, I went back to the studio and found the little old property man who had dragged a heavy carbon dioxide canister into the ring and blasted a cloud of the harmless chemical into the lion's face. I thanked him for saving my life. We talked for a while, and he said something I will always remember.

"That poor lion. He was just frightened. He thought you were going to hurt him."

The incident with Rex could very well have been the last time I was alone with a lion, and many people assumed that it would cause me to abandon my dream of working with them. It did not. In fact, if anything, it intensified that dream. Although it had never been done before, I was determined to communicate with exotic animals by making a positive emotional connection with them. I wanted to create a scenario in which the animal enjoyed what he was doing and obeyed out of affection for his human friend, and a deep respect for him. I wanted to create a working relationship between humans and animals that was based on trust.

And I knew that the biggest challenge of all would be a big cat—specifically a lion.

Most cats—big or small—are loners by nature. In the wild, leopards, jaguars, lions, and many other exotic cats live in solitude, coming together only to mate. Once that desire is slaked, they go back to being alone. Cats don't seem to *need* one another.

Cats were domesticated much later than horses and dogs because of the forested areas where they lived. The fact that they were able to climb trees made it harder for humans to approach them. Although domesticated cats do show affection to their human friends, every cat's human is familiar with the feeling that he's just being used for shelter, food, and a comfy place to sleep.

I do think evolution is making domestic cats more affectionate, but it is still the case that if you're not providing adequate accommodations, a cat will find someone who can, regardless of your affection for one another. Even the most domesticated cat brings many of its wild ways with it. Cats don't take commands the way dogs do, and they remain fiercely independent, even when they're sharing a small space. It's one of the things I like best about them, but it can also make them difficult to communicate with.

In my heart of hearts, I knew that the key to communication between animals and humans was to approach them with love, not fear, and I knew that if I could accomplish that with a lion, I'd prove my theory.

All I needed was that lion.

2

The warm, gentle breeze hugged the earth, drying elephant grass damp from the morning's mist. All was still on the African veldt. The early sun meant that it was time to gather their kin and drink from the cool water bubbling from the underground springs, but it also signaled a time of caution. Sentinels from each species stood on duty, watching, ready to sound the alarm if need be.

A large full-bellied lioness lay in the deep grass under a low-lying umbrella acacia tree, just out of reach of the hot morning sun. A slightly smaller male lay perhaps fifty feet away, hidden in the grass, as motionless as a stone, his stomach filled with the same meal.

Breakfast had been an easy kill, over in a matter of seconds. The lone young wildebeest never saw them coming. Listening to the voice of nature that bound them together, the lions had sprung as one, precise, unified. The wildebeest died instantly; the male's huge paw had broken its neck.

On a nearby mound, two pairs of eyes peered from above a broken piece of decayed candelabrum tree. They were the cubs of the female, six weeks old. Their father had lost the battle with this new male. He had left, bloody and torn, to lick his wounds and then to seek out another lioness to start another family.

The new male had not taken kindly to the cubs. The lioness launched a full-out attack against him whenever he showed aggression toward them, or the cubs wouldn't have stood a chance. She was larger than he was, and vicious when her babies were threatened.

The carcass of the wildebeest lay between the adults and the cubs. The grotesque rib cage and eyeless skull were left as offerings to the vultures, who waited their turn, high in the yellow fever trees.

The cubs, too, smelled the warm blood of the dead wildebeest, and saliva dripped from their lips. Although they were too young to eat the meat, their instincts were already kicking in, and they longed to wet their tiny muzzles with the source of the delicious smell.

The male stretched and yawned, skin pulled taut over his full, round belly. He licked his bloody paws, eyes closed, enjoying the feel of his tongue against his skin.

The cubs had been commanded by their mother to stay put, but they were irresistibly drawn by the tantalizing, warm smell coming from the kill site. They crept forward slowly, nostrils filled with the scent, anxious to get close, and lick, maybe even tear a bit of skin off the carcass. Their mother had never left them alone so long after a kill. Had she forgotten? Their stomachs ached with hunger, and the smell made them even more desperate to nurse.

Their motion caught the male's eye. He stopped his cleaning, his tongue stilled by a thought: these weren't his cubs, not from his seed. He looked at the lioness. She lay motionless on her back, belly to the sky.

A primitive instinct overcame him. His eyes widened, and the furrows of his brow deepened as he looked again at the little cubs. To him, they weren't cute. He didn't care that they were kin to his race. He felt no paternal emotions toward them at all. He simply saw another lion's offspring. They would grow and have cubs of their own and his territory would once again be threatened.

He got to his feet and walked toward them, stiff-legged.

When the cubs saw their new father coming toward them, they hid in the bush, half snarling and half purring, not sure. The female cub's ears flashed back and forth. Father or predator? Their mother was still lying belly-up. The big male advanced to within a few feet of the girl cub, and she, more eager than her brother for the security her new father could bring, decided to trust this new lion.

The big male looked down at her, his expression completely passive. Then, with a lunge, he grabbed her by the head and with a sharp crunch, squashed her little skull. The cub dangled from his mouth, twitching, then terribly still. He relaxed his jaw, letting the tiny body slip from his mouth to the ground. He raised his head, pressing his tongue to the roof of his mouth. Wrinkling his lips, he grimaced, smelling and tasting the cub's essence, acknowledging his heritage and feeling his own strength.

Now his gaze fell on the little male, trembling from what he had seen. The cub's eyes were enormous, and urine soaked his tail. The huge lion moved in his direction, and the cub backed away under an acacia bush, snarling.

Finally the lioness heard the cub's distress and sat up, alert, immediately smelling danger. The male, claws extended, lunged for the cub, one enormous paw swiping under the bush. The cub, shaking with fear, backed even deeper under the thorns.

His mother was in the air, and in two bounds, she'd hit the male, knocking his hind legs out from under him. He whipped around, snarling his fury. She was bigger than he, but he was defending his territory now, and she was no match for his onslaught. Forced to back down, she slunk away, and the male turned to finish what he had started.

But the little male cub was gone, racing full tilt back through the wait-a-bit bush, its thorns ripping and tearing at his body. He kept running, tripping, falling over boulders, sliding on the loose gravel beds. He ran for his life.

The male did not give chase. The cub was gone, and he was content—perhaps because he knew that the cub's chance of surviving without his mother was slim. The cub's mother settled back down, resigned. Her new mate had done what his instinct told him to do—kill another male's offspring to make room for his own.

The cub didn't know that he wasn't being pursued, and so he kept running, far away from everything he'd ever known in his short life. The only home he'd ever known had been the rolling vistas of the grasslands on the veldt. Weeks before, he had watched the last of the menacing rain clouds form in the distant hills, sweeping across the open spaces of the savannah. Silently they had drifted toward his family. It had scared him when the sky darkened, the warm sultry wind blowing in advance, drying the ground against the onslaught of the rain. The animals had moved, putting the trees and bushes between them and the soon-to-be deluge. Droplets of early rain sprinkled the earth, and dust-covered raindrops beaded on the ground. Lightning cracked across the sky, followed by the ominous sound of thunder. The cubs had pushed down under their mother, down where the heat of her body took away the worry, where the noise of the storm could barely be heard.

Those chilly winter storms had left the plains verdant, with lush emeralds and lime greens, and he had spent his early life playing there. But now the little cub found himself in inhospitable territory, a dry, mountainous, brush-covered region. It was far too soon for him to be out on his own. He needed protection, shelter, and above all, the warmth and nourishment that only his mother could provide. And he missed his sister. He whined plaintively as he tripped his way through the scrubby underbrush.

Predators were everywhere. Hyenas, jackals, tawny eagles—practically everything that moved was a danger to something so small. The cub knew of predators, not by name or sight, but by the way his mother's body hardened when they were near. Perhaps his lion smell would keep them away. But he didn't know to creep in the bushes when a jackal appeared, or to stay still when an eagle made lazy circles above him, or to lie in a deserted warthogs' burrow until the yelp of the hyena was far away.

Though he was scratched, thin, and weak, he was driven by his own powerful survival instinct to continue.

Soon a cool breeze and a powerful roar signaled that he'd reached the mighty Zambezi River. Winding its way through the canyons, the river opened up into a small valley, spreading wide and shallow across the flat terrain. The cub, exhausted and dehydrated, staggered down a ravine into the water and sank down among the water greens. In a hurry to slurp the cool water, he dropped his head beneath the surface and filled his nostrils, setting off a spasm of coughing. Too much too soon. After a bit, he steadied himself enough to drink without coughing. A breeze cooled his fevered body.

He lay flat, stretched out in a shallow place, his chin lying on the sandy bottom, water up to the edge of his nose. The current swirled around him. Small bands of "water-walker" spiders skipped past on their spindly legs. Looking for something to ease his hunger pangs, he sucked on some bitter water plants. They brought foam to his lips, then a wrenching, spasmodic heaving. Whatever little nourishment was left in his stomach was vomited out and swept away with the current.

The minutes turned into hours, and the hot African sun began to take its toll. The cub wandered down the riverbank on bloodied paws, searching for a spot of shade. As he rounded a bend, he saw a blurred movement through his bloodshot, drooping eyes. He felt warmth coming from the shape. His feverish mind saw his mother, heard her calling, ready to lick his wounds and fill his tummy with warm, life-giving milk.

He opened his mouth to let out a cry, but no sound came out. His head bobbled on his thin shoulders as he ran, falling, toward the warm blur, and collapsed at its feet. It was a woman, and as she gathered him up as his mother once had, he felt as safe and secure as he had in his mother's paws. His soft muzzle nudged her warm skin, looking for a nipple. As he began to lose consciousness, his small mouth nursed a finger. He couldn't understand why there wasn't any milk.

3

 There are events that change the entire course of your life. The event that changed mine forever started with a phone call from friends I hadn't heard from for a long time.

It was the mid-1950s, and I was living on a ranch in the Santa Monica Hills. I was making a living renting animals to the movies and working as a stuntman. I had also built a reputation as a conservationist, and lectured often on the future of exotic animals at various animal nonprofits, universities, and conferences.

It was my belief then, as it is now, that the human species' consistent refusal to treat animals and their habitats with decency and respect will inevitably have one unhappy result: the extinction of those animals. I am an extremely optimistic person. I tend to see the glass not half full, or half empty, but overflowing. But I am sorry to say that I do not have a great deal of faith in my fellow man, especially when it comes to our animal brethren, and I have spent much of my career trying to bring the world's attention to this issue—before it is too late.

In the early fifties, during a symposium on endangered species at the University of California at Davis, one of the finest veterinary schools in the world, I had met a wonderful couple, Jack and Brini. Jack was a rather handsome Englishman, tall and a bit on the thin side, with graying temples, a slight mustache, and a mild accent. Brini, also British, had been raised in the United States. She was a tanned blond, with just a hint of an accent and a truly terrific smile. They had met when she was at Stanford University, and had married a year later.

They were studying animal conservation, which was how they ended up at my lecture on the survival instinct, and the three of us hit it off immediately. We agreed completely about animals and their predicaments, and we spent lots of time after the seminar discussing our thoughts on these topics.

"I think human overpopulation is the primary cause of the depletion of our natural reserves," Brini said during dinner on our last evening. "Where are these animals supposed to live, once we've destroyed their habitats? It's their territory, for heaven's sake."

"Don't get started, Brini," Jack warned. But I was as passionate about the subject as she was, and the conversation went on late into the night. Sure that I was among like-minded souls, I shared my desire to have and train an African lion using positive emotional training techniques, and to build a relationship based on trust and respect. "I would love to be able to establish a way of communicating that would bring our two species closer together," I told Brini and Jack. I spoke at length about my budding theories, and they agreed that it would be a wonderful experiment.

We'd parted friends, and sent periodic postcards from our various travels, but we hadn't seen each other in years. Then, suddenly, I received that life-changing long-distance phone call from Jack.

"Something odd happened to us when we were on safari, Ralph," he'd said.

A week or two later, on a quiet, sunny morning in early April, I stood on top of a hill at my ranch, looking down into the open country below. The sky was the most brilliant blue, and the sweet scent of spring flowers drifted up from the valley. I had never seen a more beautiful day in more beautiful country. Adrenaline charged through my body when I spotted the spiraling dust from a truck speeding up from the valley below. It turned onto the dirt road leading to our ranch.

Today my lion was coming.

A red-tailed hawk, flying high, shrieked a welcome to Jack and Brini as the pickup truck came to a halt.

We greeted each other with heartfelt hugs, feeling as comfortable as if we had been separated by mere days, not years.

"This dust reminds me a bit of Africa," said Brini with a smile, smacking some of it off her trousers.

"Someday I will venture there," I said. "I truly believe it is the cradle of mankind, and I know one has to look back to see the future."

"Yes, indeed." Brini smiled. "Our safari was unbelievable. We spent three weeks traveling through Zambia, Tanzania, and Kenya, photographing Cape buffalo, African lions, rhinos, elephants, and leopards—what hunters refer to as the big five." The excitement in her voice was infectious. It was as if she were back in Africa, experiencing it all again firsthand.

"Ralph, there is an energy there that permeates one's whole being. The country is beautiful—the veldt, well, I never imagined there were so many shades of green. It was just after the rains, and the herds of wildebeest, impala, and zebra were everywhere. Thousands of them! And we must have seen four or five prides of lions."

The mention of the lions reminded us all why they were at the ranch.

"The ranger told us that what happened to us on the Zambezi River had never happened before," she said.

"He said the cub was at the point of collapse when Brini came upon him. He wouldn't have lasted another hour," added Jack.

"I'm surprised he let you take the cub out of the country," I said. Even then, there were stringent laws preventing people from taking any animals out of Africa.

"I think he knew that if the cub had any chance at all of surviving, it would be with Brini. She stayed up every night for a week, feeding him, keeping him warm," said Jack.

"He would lie on my chest all night and most of the day during the time he was healing, and I think that more than anything, the bodily contact was what saved him. He could hear my heartbeat and feel me breathe, and my body heat kept him warm. It's what his mother would have done," said Brini.

"Did he make the trip back okay?" I asked anxiously, shifting my eyes to the cage in the back of the pickup.

"Splendidly," said Jack. "You must be anxious to meet your new friend."

We walked back to the truck. Jack undid the chain and lowered the tailgate. The cage was wrapped in canvas with a few ropes securing it to the side of the truck. Undoing the knots, he started to uncover the cage.

"If you don't mind," I said, putting my hand on his arm, "I would like to have our first meeting in private."

The couple smiled, nodding their understanding.

"We call him Zamba," said Brini. "After the river where we found him."

"And so it shall be," I said. "It's a fitting name."

"Yes, well, I guess we should be going," offered Jack.

"No coffee?" I asked, although I could barely breathe, looking at the covered cage.

"We have to get back." Brini's eyes filled with tears. "I'm really going to miss him," she said, taking my hands in hers. "You know, when I first held him in my arms, I was thinking of you. When we first met, you spoke of wanting a lion of your own. I can't explain it, but I knew this would be the lion you have been waiting to share your life with. You're the best person for Zamba, Ralph."

Her kindness embarrassed me, but my heart filled with appreciation. I touched the cage. "I can't begin to tell you how I feel at this moment, and how moved I am that you thought of me after all these years," I told her. I could feel the slight burn of tears welling in my own eyes. "I really have been waiting my whole life for this moment."

Brini's British reserve kicked in. "I guess we had better be going," she said quietly. She had said her good-byes to Zamba earlier; best not to repeat. She could cry in the car. Jack lifted the little bundle to the ground. No sound came from the cage.

I hugged them good-bye.

"Thanks. Thank you so very much."

A handshake from Jack, and they were gone.

I picked up the small cage and climbed the short distance to the crest of the hill, where there was a giant oak tree. It must have been at least four hundred years old, and although it had been ravaged by centuries of storms and natural disasters, it still stood tall and majestic. It was the largest and most beautiful tree in the county, and it could be seen for miles in all directions.

This tree had become a legend in the area, and she was affectionately referred to as the Old Lady. Her lowest branches, long and heavy with foliage, hung in a huge circle, tips bending until they touched the earth. Witches' hair moss hung from the branches. The growth was so thick that one could neither see in, nor get close to her trunk. When she shed her leaves, they fell still green and full of energy, an emerald carpet encircling the matriarch.

Everyone who saw her immediately recognized the feeling of a cathedral about her, and in fact many church groups gathered around her for special services. I was fortunate and proud to have inherited her on the property.

In years past, whenever I had felt alone, confused, or wounded, I had gone to her, seeking direction. I have always believed in nature as the true way to reach one's God, and the Old Lady offered me a natural temple and gave me an opportunity to recharge.

You could drive up the hill close to where the Old Lady stood, but the best way to approach her was by a small trail starting in the valley below. It twisted its way over cascading streams into a thick medieval forest, lush with conifers and giant-leaved plants. The forest was filled with mule deer, cottontail rabbits, gray tree squirrels, and the occasional raccoon and opossum. In the creek beds, shy newts and pink salamanders hid under moss-covered rocks. To end up at the base of the Old Lady after such a walk really made you feel that the oak was nature's church.

Very few people knew about a small opening in the low-lying branches around the back of the tree, hidden by a thick patch of manzanita brush. I picked my way through the opening, carrying the cage and its precious cargo. Once through, it was cool and quiet inside, an amphitheater filled with the intoxicating smell of the damp, rich, reddish earth. The gnarled base of the tree trunk was huge, and there were no initials cut into its bark. It was as pure as the day its seed sprang into life.

I stood there, full with the realization that this was a moment I had been waiting for all my life. All was quiet. I set the cage down in the middle of the circle and sat with my back against the tree, where the lowest branches were high enough for a man to stand at full height.

The silence was broken by an impatient "aghruh" from inside the cage.

I walked over and gently unwrapped the canvas. The cage was made with loosely fitted wooden slats, with a wire screen on the front. I reached down and undid the door latch and let it swing open, and then I went back to where I had been sitting, with my back against the tree. The morning sunlight shone through the slats, casting beams of golden light across a pair of huge, beautiful, unblinking eyes.

I said "Zamba?" as softly as I could.

The cage moved. The cub got to his feet and peered out the door.

Such a face! It was truly a face of God's making. Perfect, trusting, and so very beautiful. We looked at each other for a while. I was practically overcome with the joy of it all.

"Aghruh!" he said.

"Hi," I said.

He stood there, head up, standing as tall as he could, planning his next step. Then, with an air of dignity, he started toward me. He had all the features of an adult in miniature. When he got a few feet away, he stopped and looked directly at me again.

Extending my arms, I said, "Hi, Zamba."

He tilted his head, waited a single beat, and then ambled right into my arms. Although he was barely two months old, his little body bowled me over—not with his strength, but with his pure enthusiasm. I lay back on the ground while his small pink tongue licked every inch of my face; he nursed my nose until it was red. He found my tears of joy and licked them away. Then, hugging my neck with his soft paws, he collapsed on my chest, got comfortable, and fell asleep with his face on mine. We didn't move for the next two hours. My Zamba was home.

4

In the years before Zamba came to me, I had been developing a philosophy of training animals that was based on love, not fear. This system would eventually become known as affection training, and I don't think I'm overstating the case when I say that it revolutionized the way animals are trained and treated in the motion picture industry.

The system evolved over a long period of time. In fact, the first seeds of the idea of affection training were planted on the day of my eighth birthday.

"Wake up, birthday boy." My mother's voice penetrated my sleep. "Happy birthday!" She leaned over and kissed me on the cheek.

Reluctantly I left my beautiful dream. It was a dream that I'd had over and over again since I was a very small child.

In this dream, heavy snow blanketed the silent world as I curled up on God's eyelid. The snow was beautiful, but I was chilled to the bone. A lion of massive proportions approached through the flurries, and immediately I was flooded with a sense of calm. This lion was my protector, my mentor, my friend.

He moved in slow motion, radiating a pulsating glow of warmth, and as he turned his head toward me, the warm air coming from his nostrils thawed the cold in my body. Time slowed down—every blink of his enormous eyes seemed to last an eternity as he looked deep into my being.

Then I'd wake up under a big old brown wool quilt my grandma had made years ago, and slowly the warmth the dream had imparted would leave me. We had no heat in the house until my uncle Chan and I started up the furnace each morning.

This birthday was no exception. Shivering, I quickly put on my knickers, a heavy wool shirt that itched something terrible against my cold skin, a coat, two pairs of socks, a wool skullcap, and a pair of red earmuffs. My gloves were cold and hard, so I beat them briskly against the bedpost until some of the elasticity came back. Mom gave me a thermos of hot cocoa to warm me, and I headed out the door to help my uncle Chan start the furnace.

This was my life. From birth until I was eleven years old, I lived in a place I detested. The south side of Chicago was a middle- to lower-class section of town, full of rat-infested alleyways, torn-up streets, and week-old garbage. Every day seemed colder and wetter than the day before. My parents were separated, so my mother, sister, and I lived with relatives, supplementing their charity with whatever Mother could earn from a series of small-paying jobs. I had very little contact with my father—when we did spend the day together, he'd usually drop me off at a whorehouse his brother owned so the girls could babysit me, hugging me to their huge, baby-powdered breasts. Like any child raised without a father, I wished that he had been more of a full-time presence in my life, but it was only when I became a father myself that I fully appreciated what he'd missed. I believe that both my father and I could have benefited from each other's love, but we did not see each other often enough for a real relationship to develop.

My only escape from reality was a collection of lion paraphernalia that I kept in my room. I looked every day in the newspaper and saved any advertisement or article that featured them, and over the years, my relatives had given me a few cherished figurines.

Someday, I thought, someday, I will leave here and live in Africa, a place full of trees and rivers with lions all around. It will be warm. And I will have my own lion. He will be my best friend and I will be his.

Fortunately, this birthday promised a break from my ordinary life. My mother, sister, and auntie had promised me a day at Aurora, an amusement park at the edge of the city. It was a special place full of barnyard animals, circus acts, carnival shows, rides, games, corn on the cob, and juicy hot dogs dripping with chili. I could hardly wait.

As I got out into the living room, I noticed that everyone had dressed up a little for the occasion—everyone except Uncle Chan. Mom wore her black-and-white polka-dot dress, my auntie Anne had on her new blouse with the puffed sleeves, and my sister, Sally Ann, wore a bright blue off-the-shoulder top to match her eyes. But Uncle Chan was wearing an old pair of jeans, wool scotch plaid shirt, and high-top boots.

He sat down across the room on the sofa and looked at me, the way he did whenever he was contemplating a reprimand or about to announce a change in our living conditions. I tried to make myself as inconspicuous as possible, sinking between the old sofa cushion and the armrest, and desperately tried to figure out what crime I might have accidentally committed.

"Come on, honey," said Auntie Anne, a little timidly, to her staring husband. "We don't want to miss the early morning performance."

She knew his moods could spoil things very quickly and didn't want anything to happen on my birthday.

"We're not going," came his terse reply.

His words were like a slap in the face.

"But honey, we're all ready and—"

A look from Chan quickly stopped her. She turned to me with her head tilted, a sheepish smile conveying her helplessness. My mother sat motionless, afraid to say the wrong thing.

"The boy's too old to go to some sissy-girl park. I've got him something that will turn him into a man. Here!" He reached behind his back and pulled out a tall brown-paper wrapped package.

The entire family was startled; this may have been the first gift my uncle had ever given anyone. I didn't care what it held; nothing could replace the outing I had so happily anticipated for months. I laid the package across my lap and began slowly unwrapping the paper.

"Hurry up, goddammit. We don't have all day!" he yelled. His sudden outburst startled me, and I quickly tore at the paper. As soon as the box was open, I felt sicker to my stomach than I ever had before. Lying before me was the one thing in the entire world I hated the most—a hunting rifle.

"Isn't it a beauty? I bought it brand-new from a used gun dealer. It's a 30–30, big enough to knock a hole you can see through in any good-sized deer."

I struggled to catch my breath. The rifle lay there on my lap, its long black barrel all shiny and polished. The stock was made of a light-colored wood, the same kind as their dining room table.

"Well, go ahead, pick it up," he urged.

It was almost too heavy for me to hold. I knew my uncle wanted me to try it out, point it at something as though I were going to shoot. For one wild second, I imagined pointing it at him. Instead I "shot" at the living room lamp.

"How's it feel, son?" he asked.

"Fine, Uncle—thanks."

"Tomorrow we'll go up to Three Point. It's a great place for deer this time of year. If we're lucky, we'll bring home a nice buck. Be the best birthday you'll ever have."

I spent the rest of the day in numb misery. The disappointment of the amusement park seemed a hundred years away, overshadowed completely by the threat of what the next day would bring, the gun a silent, evil reminder propped up in the corner of the living room. The night was no better: I tossed and turned, wide-eyed and feverish, unable to stop the voices in my head. Killing a deer? The man must be crazy! Why? We didn't need deer meat for food. There were always plenty of hamburgers in the refrigerator. Why kill an innocent animal? What was the purpose?

I was already up and sitting on the edge of my bed when my mother came in the next morning. She looked tired, and I knew she was worried for me. She sat on the edge of the bed and took my hands in hers as her eyes filled with tears.

"You know, honey, your uncle Chan means well. He was in the navy for many years, serving on a destroyer. He never had children of his own, and I think he always wanted to have a boy so he could teach him all the things he thinks a boy should be."

Destroyer was a good name for Uncle Chan. "Momma, I can't kill any animal, let alone a deer. They're beautiful and have families and don't hurt anybody."

Her voice was soft. "Look, honey, you know we can't afford to get our own place. What with the Depression and all, times are rough. Auntie Anne and Uncle Chan have been good to us, letting us live here. If I say something, well, you know how Uncle Chan is. He could ask us to leave, and what would we do then?"

I was still hoping against hope that she'd tell me I didn't have to go. "Please tell me I don't have to kill a deer."

"No, of course not. I just want you to know that things are difficult now and I don't want them to get any worse." Her hands were clasped in her lap, and by now, her voice was barely audible. "You're a good boy, Ralphie, and I know you'll make the right decision."

When she hugged me I felt her tears on my cheek.

My new rifle lay in its carrying case on the backseat of the Chevy, nestled up next to Uncle Chan's. We had been driving about three hours, the city left behind us, when the old truck broke down. Uncle Chan said it was the carburetor, and siphoned some gas out of the tank into a Coke bottle. The hood was split down the center, and he raised it on one side, exposing the engine. He lifted me up onto the front fender, showing me how to slowly drip gas from the bottle into the carburetor. In order for the truck to continue to run, I had to balance on the fender, dripping gas, while we drove.

"Don't drip it on the engine, boy. You'll blow us all to kingdom come."

He drove quite slowly, as I balanced and dripped. It was a warm day, and the breeze felt good blowing in my face, and although my task made me a bit uncomfortable, at least it kept me from thinking of where we were going. The drive was beautiful, and the forest surrounded us with all its awesome splendor. I felt at home there—I knew that a place like this was where all my hopes and dreams for the future lay. But given the day's objective, instead of comforting me, the smells and the sounds coming from the surrounding forest only intensified my dread.

I couldn't look around much because if the drip wasn't steady, the engine would cough and sputter. It happened once, and a look from my uncle ensured that it didn't happen again. I knew if I let some of the gas drip on the hot engine the whole truck could catch fire, and I gave it serious thought, but ultimately I didn't have the nerve. We arrived at our destination intact.

Uncle Chan parked the truck under a large oak. He took the rifles from their cases and leaned them against the tree, then opened one of the boxes of bullets he'd brought, grabbed a handful, and dumped them into my pocket. From another box he dug out a bunch of larger shells for his rifle and filled his pocket to the brim. He donned a red cap and put another on me, which covered my ears. I had to pull my ears out and fold them over the top so I could hear.

For the next half hour my uncle showed me how to load, aim, and fire the rifle with the precision of a master. He made me repeat every move four or five times until he was satisfied that I had it down. Despite my anxiety and loathing, I had a moment of wishing that we shared some interests. He would have been a good teacher.

He strapped on his bowie hunting knife, hung a pair of binoculars around his neck, and we were off. I had been hoping all day that we wouldn't see any deer at all, and now I started praying in earnest. I crunched my heels into the dry leaves, hoping to scare away anything that came near until Uncle Chan walloped me on the shoulder and told me to be quiet. I watched as he took an infantry position, stalking the enemy, his gun at the ready as we headed deep into the forest.

For two hours we trekked. There was no sign of deer, or anything else for that matter, and when Uncle Chan said that maybe we'd have to come back another day, I actually began to enjoy myself. The forest was lush and beautiful, and I drank the best water I'd ever tasted from a small brook.

About two hours later, we were on our way back, crossing that same brook, when Uncle Chan suddenly froze, eyes narrowed. He grabbed my arm and pulled me to the ground.

A huge, splendid buck was drinking upstream. The noise from the bubbling water had blocked the sound of our approach. Uncle Chan belly-crawled behind a log nearby, half dragging me alongside him by my coat collar.

"Keep down!" he hissed.

I was shaking from head to toe, sure he could hear my thumping heart. Silently he took off his cap and carefully brought his rifle up over the tree, aiming it at the deer. He motioned for me to do the same, and with shaking hands, I complied.

"Adjust your sights."

Both rifles had huge sights that ran down the barrel, practically as big as the barrels themselves. As the deer came into focus, I could see just how magnificent he was. His antlers, rich with points, reached high in the air. His liquid eyes brimmed with dignity and intelligence, and the sunlight illuminated his beautiful flanks. This was the daddy of all deer. Uncle Chan edged up close to me, his whisper almost silent.

"Ease the safety off very carefully. No click!"

He looked like a madman.

"I don't want to hear a click. No click! You hear? No click!" His hand was trembling.

I nodded. I put my hand over the safety. There was no click. The deer, after he'd finished his drink, stood like the prince he was, looking into the forest and assuring himself that all was well. His nose sniffed the air, but we were upwind. He knew nothing of us.

"Now, lock your sights and aim where his heart is. Just to the right of his shoulder joint where it meets the body."

I couldn't stop looking at the buck's stunning head, with the touch of white around his quivering nose and his crown of horns.

His eyes were the most beautiful things I had ever seen, and I felt as sure as I had ever been about anything that God had given this deer those eyes to see the beauty of what He had created. If I shot this deer, it would be like shooting God.

Uncle Chan was so close I could feel his lips on my ear, smell the coffee on his breath.

"When you ease that trigger back, do it slowly, you hear?" he rasped. I nodded. "Brace the butt of the gun tight to your shoulder. It's got a kick."

In my head, I was screaming at the deer, *Run, please, run!* and yet the weight of the gun was still against my shoulder. I was just eight years old, and this man was as close to a father as any I'd known. As much as I loved that deer, I also desperately wanted my uncle's approval, wanted him to think I was brave and strong. If I didn't take the shot, what would happen to us? My mother worked so hard to pay our share at the apartment, I knew she could never afford one of our own. I put my finger on the trigger.

"What are you waiting for? Do it! Do it, you stupid boy—do it now!"

I pulled the trigger. The explosion was like thunder breaking in the quiet of the forest. The bullet arched toward the deer.

In one move, the expert that he was, my uncle stood up in full view, rifle at the ready, and fired one shot through the heart of the buck. I had deliberately shot so that my bullet lodged in a tree behind.

I hadn't been able to do it, but it didn't matter. The prince was dead.

"You stupid, stupid son of a bitch!"

My uncle sent a resounding slap across my face, knocking me to the ground.

"Get up, you coward. GET UP!" I scrambled to my feet, stumbling from a wave of dizziness, in time to see him unsheath his bowie knife.

He's going to kill me! I thought. How would he explain my death to my mother? "Please, Uncle Chan, please don't do this. I'm sorry. Truly I am. Please don't kill me."

Tears flowed freely down my face, and hot urine ran down my leg. I was shaking all over.

He handed me the knife and dragged me by the arm toward the dead deer, pushing me hard until I fell on the body. I felt his warmth, and his body smelled like the forest itself.

"Skin that deer," he roared.

He pointed to the spot where I was to start. My hand was shaking so badly that it took three tries before I could even puncture the skin. As soon as I made the cut, the innards belched forth. Stomach. Intestines. There was blood everywhere. I wiped the tears from my face and smeared blood across my cheek. This is God's blood, I thought. The stench was unbearable. I vomited over and over. I tried to get up but slipped in the blood. Finally, mercifully, my mind went blank. My whole system wound down and shut off, and I was in shock.

To this day, I don't know how I completed the task that my uncle had set before me. The blood on my face dried, with no more tears to smear it. The deer's skin came free of the body. The head stayed with the antlers. The whole time, his dull, lifeless eyes, now covered in blood and slime, were fixed on me.

We draped the skin over the hood of the car and tied the antlers on the front—a hood ornament. The meat was cut into quarters and wrapped for the freezer back home.

I peeled off my clothes and stood naked while my uncle poured buckets of cold water over me from the stream. I wasn't even embarrassed for him to see my nakedness. All of my dignity was already gone. Like the deer, I was dead.

5

After that horrible day hunting with Uncle Chan, I pledged my life to a crusade against animal cruelty. Whether it's changing the way animals are trained for the movies, or raising awareness about conserving their habitats in the wild, I have been on that crusade every day since.

Still, you're probably wondering how a passionate but poor boy from Chicago's South Side ended up in Hollywood, surrounded by lions and tigers and chimpanzees and elephants. How did I accomplish my dream?

You certainly wouldn't have known to look at me that I'd grow up to share my life with exotic animals. I was an introverted child. Small for my age, with a thick bush of curly hair and glasses, I stayed in the background, unnoticed and inconspicuous most of the time. But I don't remember a time when I wasn't completely obsessed with exotics, and my encounter with the deer only deepened my love of all things wild. There was never a doubt in my mind that I wanted to work with animals, especially exotic ones, when I grew up. My career has always felt less like a choice than the fulfillment of a destiny.

The snow lion dream, which would recur throughout my life, was not my only childhood lion dream. When I was about ten years old, I had a dream that gave me a goal that I would spent the rest of my life trying to achieve: honest, open, and—dare I say it?— loving communication between animals and humans.

In the dream, I was walking in the alley behind our house in Chicago. Every minute detail was clear; I could smell the stink of the rotting garbage, hear the women yelling to one another as they put their laundry on the lines. I felt afraid, as I did in real life; cats and rabid rats battled for meat in these alleys, and the cats didn't always win.

At the end of the alley, though, there was a bright light, and I walked as fast as I could toward it. Soon I reached a hilly meadow area, carpeted in scented grass and filled with scattered trees, illu- minated by the cleanest and most beautiful light I had ever seen. And everywhere in the hills were different animals, all kinds— tigers and antelopes and giraffes—sleeping and grazing and play- ing with one another. It was truly idyllic, the most beautiful place I had ever seen.

Directly in front of me, there was a massive tree with a miracle underneath it—a full-grown lion with a gorgeous mane, and sleep- ing cuddled into his side, a baby lamb. I approached the two of them, and I was flooded with a truly astonishing feeling of accep- tance and love. As the lion watched, I knelt down to pet the lamb, filled with the overwhelming sensation that this was my true fam- ily. I had come home.

It felt less like a dream than a visitation, to be honest, and I can still remember every single detail to this day. It's a biblical image, although I didn't know that then. Whatever it was, it had an incredibly profound effect on me, and I was more sure than ever that I would find a way to spend my life with exotic animals.

In my eleventh year, I inched just a little bit closer to realizing my impossible dream. That was the year we moved to Southern California.

My dad had called, trying to patch things up with my mother one last time, and she went for it. So I, my mother, aunt and uncle, sister, along with Polly the parrot (the very beginning of my animal collections), drove to Southern California in Chan's beat-up old truck. It took almost two weeks (we had no fewer than ten flat tires on the way out), and when we got there, we found my dad shacked up with another woman, but we decided to say good-bye to Chan and Anne, find our own place, and see what California had to offer anyway—and I've been there ever since.

As far as I'm concerned, it was in California that my life really began, because that's when my life with animals started in earnest. For the first time, I was breathing fresh air instead of smog and car exhaust. I could go to the zoo, hike in the Hollywood Hills, and above all, have the freedom to keep a real collection of creepy-crawlies in my room.

The comedienne Carol Burnett grew up in our building. She was my best friend and, for a time, my girl. The neighborhood was rough, and home wasn't always happy for either one of us. She got a kick out of helping me catch snakes and other things that go bump in the night. We would sneak off to the hills and spend hours on our bellies, catching and studying and collecting various creatures. Nothing teaches like experience, and I got a great education in snakes and insects—an education that would serve me well working these animals later in my life.

. . .

I had my first real job working with animals when I was in junior high school. It was a part-time job at a pet shop called the Hollywood Aquarium, and I was paid seventy-five cents an hour—not a lot of money, but every little bit helped at home. And although the pay was rotten, I felt fortunate to get any kind of a job working with animals.

The owner was Sylvester Chichester Lloyd, a bespectacled man with a large stomach, in his late sixties. He always wore the same style of clothes, khaki suspenders over a khaki shirt and pants.

My job was to clean all the cages: guinea pigs, mice, white rats, snakes, lizards, and birds. I was also "allowed" to change all the filters in the fish tanks when they needed to be cleaned, and I even helped feed a live goldfish to a piranha once a day.

Mr. Lloyd had little or no interest in the welfare of the animals who paid his bills. One morning I found our large boa constrictor nearly dead. He was a prominent fixture in the store, and been featured in a large cage right as you walked into the shop.

"The boa's dying, Mr. Lloyd," I said quietly, figuring he'd find a way to blame me. The truth was that the snake had been sick for months and hadn't accepted food since I had started working there. Its scales were dull, and it had slimy yellow mucus oozing from its mouth.

Mr. Lloyd ignored me.

"Shouldn't we call a vet?" I asked.

"No," said Mr. Lloyd, without looking up from his paper, "too expensive. It would cost more than the snake is worth."

"What should I do with it?"

"Leave it. It looks good for the customers. They don't know it's sick. Even if it dies, well, just leave it. It won't stink for a week. Nobody will know."

• • •

Occasionally a call would come in to Hollywood Aquarium from the studios asking for snakes, white rats, a fish tank setup, or even one of our beautiful cockatoos to work in a scene, and sometimes I helped to carry the equipment. This was my first taste of Hollywood, and I was fascinated by the glamour I saw on the sets. The lights were bright, and the women were gorgeous, and I would stare for as long as I could at the artificial scenery: the snow-covered Alps, a lush jungle, New York's neon-lit Times Square. To my surprise, even Chicago's elevated trains were represented.

Mr. Lloyd took a call one morning from a studio asking to rent some scorpions. When he was finished, he turned to me.

"Ralph, my boy, tomorrow is your big day. They want me to work a couple of our scorpions in a movie and I am going to, uh, allow you to do the job. My back's been acting up a bit, and all that bending over will only irritate it. If you do a good job I'll give you a ten-cent raise, bringing you up to eighty-five cents an hour! How about that?"

I knew he was afraid to touch them or he would have done the job himself. Thank God I had already gone through my apprenticeship with bugs, both splashing around Chicago's Gory Creek with my friend Leon and an *Amateur's Guide to Snakes and Reptiles,* and later with Carol in the Hollywood Hills. My experience had taught me that although these big black scorpions looked terrifying, their sting was no more serious than a bee's. They were actually very easy to work with.

And they were in great demand. Before the advent of computer graphics, the industry referred to a certain kind of movie as a "special effects" film, and we were the special effects. If they needed a mammoth dinosaur or colossal alien creature, they took an image of an exotic animal like a lizard or a scorpion and enlarged it against a special background, lending the "monster" the illusion of incredible size, power, and strength. Sometimes it would be necessary to "dress" our monsters, which meant adding claws, fangs, scales, extra tongues—all easier said than done on a miniature scale.

This particular scene was supposed to be a battle between two monsters. My job was to hold two scorpions by their stinger tails and have them fight each other. Then I turned them loose in a large sand pit so the camera could see their raised stingers. The animals "fought" by locking their claws together, which didn't hurt them in the least. That was it—we were done. Eventually they'd enlarge the film so my scorpions looked bigger than an apartment building.

The producer gave me a five-dollar tip. I couldn't believe it! I wondered all the way home if I should tell Mr. Lloyd about the tip, but I knew that if I did, he would take it from me. My mother could buy a week's supply of food with that money.

So ended my first studio job. I didn't know then that providing Hollywood with exotic animals would become my livelihood for many years to come.

I learned a lot at Hollywood Aquarium. Mr. Lloyd was the first person I'd met who used animals for his own personal gain without any thought for their welfare. Unfortunately, he wouldn't be the last. I was to learn, over the next many years in the animal business, that not everyone who works with animals is motivated by love. And it was from Mr. Lloyd that I learned you can tell a lot about the way a person will treat the humans in his life from the way he treats the animals.

One day I sold a customer a scarlet macaw. It cost him three hundred dollars. That was a big sale—probably the biggest Mr. Lloyd had seen in some time, and I was due for a big tip. He had promised that on any sales over fifty dollars, he would give me "something nice."

"My boy, today I'm taking you to lunch. You deserve that after making such a big sale."

Lunch! I didn't want lunch. I wanted some money so I could buy things that were needed at home. But I didn't protest, and at noon he locked up the store and put out the CLOSED FOR LUNCH sign. We headed for the drugstore on the corner and sat at the counter. I wanted a Salisbury steak.

"No, no, boy. Get something special. How about liver and onions? It comes with French fries." He seemed to know a lot about the dish. "Give us liver and onions and a roast beef plate."

While the food was being prepared I went to call my mom. She had been sick for a few days, and my sister and I had finally ganged up on her and gotten her to stay home from work. When I hung up the phone, a piece of paper came out of the refund slot and with it a bunch of change—a whole handful. I was delighted!

"Look at this, Mr. Lloyd. The telephone emptied all this change after my call."

Mr. Lloyd eyed the coins as though they were gold.

"Give them here, boy. You're still on the clock, so that change is mine," he said, scooping the coins from my hand. "Here, keep this for your call." He left a nickel in my palm.

"You going to drink this?" Lloyd pointed to my glass of drinking water.

"I don't think so, " I said. It was a good thing, since Mr. Lloyd promptly removed his false teeth and put them in *my* drinking water! The fake teeth stared at me all through lunch, and I spent the meal helplessly watching food particles float to the top of the glass. I noticed people at the tables nearby inching their chairs away.

During the meal, I attempted to put a newspaper that I found on the counter between the teeth and me so I didn't have to look at them. I had only stopped eating for a moment when Mr. Lloyd reached over and sliced off a big chunk of my food for himself. Now I knew why he'd ordered for me.

I worked for Mr. Sylvester Chichester Lloyd during my summer vacations throughout the rest of high school, and I never did get that raise.

By the time I was in my teens, I had a fair collection of my own animals, and was making money on the side by renting them out to Hollywood productions. My mother's faith in me was unfailing, and her support unwavering—until the dozen rattlesnakes I had collected for a Kirk Douglas movie escaped from my room. Carol found the last one pinned under the broom of a very pregnant, very upset woman on the third floor. After that, Mom suggested that I find alternate housing for my creatures.

My uncle Irv, one of the sweetest men on the planet, and his family had preceded us to California. He and I went into business together, opening a pet store of our own called Nature's Haven. Irv was a bookie, so he came up with the money, and I handled the animal end of the operation. Sometimes our worlds collided. Irv used the back room of the shop to take bets, and I remember hearing him trying to keep his cool on a phone call as I scrambled after a monkey that had escaped and was rampaging through the shop.

The superstar Cornel Wilde, who was in so many of the Cecil B. DeMille pictures, was a big animal lover, and he came in all the time. I think it was largely because of him that our movie rental business really took off. The prop guy would call and say, "I need a raccoon," and I'd pack up the animal and go over and do the shot.

Often they'd need a stuntman to double the actor and work with the animal, and I was always happy to oblige. I'm small and wiry, and, happily, that body type was shared by many of the leading men of the day. I was on a special work-school program, which meant four hours of school, four hours of work. In reality, it meant four hours of school, four hours of work delivering newspapers or manning an Orange Julius stand, and four hours at the pet shop. I'd get home with just enough energy to eat dinner and listen to *I Love a Mystery* or *The Shadow* on the radio before bed. I certainly wasn't complaining. I was able to help support my family, and my dream had come true—I was making a living working with animals.

After two years, I was ready to move on. With my sister Sally Ann's help, I opened up Nature's Haven: Wild Animal Rentals on a two-acre piece of property in Van Nuys, California. It had been a dog- and cat-boarding kennel, so it was well-suited for my use.

I slowly built my collection to include raccoons, various monkeys, deer, hawks, and an impressive variety of snakes, and we were getting more and more work from the studios. I was beginning to experiment with my own self-taught methods of training them. I never used violence or deprivation or any other of the cruelty-based methods I would later learn were standard with other trainers. It simply never occurred to me.

6

Though I was happy running Nature's Haven, I found that I was still powerfully drawn to the big exotic animals. During that time, I often traveled to Thousand Oaks, a city near Los Angeles and home to the world-famous Jungleland.

Most of the animals used in the film industry and circus world were kept there, and it gave me my first exposure to the big exotics. Jungleland had started out as the World Jungle Compound, owned and operated by Louis Gobel. It was later sold to Roy Cabot, who changed the name to Jungleland and opened it to the public.

I wanted desperately to know how these animals were trained, so I volunteered to help the keepers maintain their charges. Sometimes I was allowed to help the trainers unload the animals when they were coming back from a studio job. In the end, most of what I learned was what *not* to do.

In those days, training through violence and coercion was the norm. There were no regulatory bodies like the ASPCA monitoring how working animals were trained and kept. The trainers used force to dominate the animals, and the terrified animals became even more violent in response. It was a vicious circle, one that was dangerous for both the humans and the animals involved.

Different trainers called their methods by different names, but it all boiled down to the same thing: a combination of reward and fear. If the trainers relied only on a reward to get the animal to perform, they would run into trouble when the animal's tummy was full. Since the studios lost tens of thousands of dollars a day when the animals didn't perform, the trainers were made acutely aware of how important it was for the animals to do their stunts when and how they were told to do them. So the policy was "do it—or else."

Violence was rampant, and always just out of sight. Animals were tied in inconspicuous places and beaten until they submitted to the trainer's wishes. Chimps were taken out of sight into the toilet "to teach them a lesson." The beatings were done so that they didn't leave bruises—at least any that would show on camera.

But it was at Jungleland that I met Mabel Stark. Mabel was the only woman who worked big cats in the arena in North America. She had been working big cats for most of her life, and when I knew her, she was in her late seventies. Still, she gave a performance six days a week with her ten Bengal tigers. Her training method was many years ahead of its time, and it made an enormous impression on me.

Mabel was different from the other trainers. In content, sure, her act was similar to many of the others. The cats did rollovers, sit-ups, snarls, and all the standard routines. The difference was that she treated them affectionately, hugging and talking with them. Instead of cowering in fear or raging, her cats always seemed to enjoy what they were doing. Mabel never used a weapon; she carried nothing but a short stick, which she never raised in anger. If one of the cats made an error—went to the wrong pedestal, for instance, or refused to jump a barrel—she would simply "spank" him with a touch from her little stick on his nose.

"Naughty, naughty! Now you just go back there and do it right."

She didn't care if her schoolmistress routine interrupted her act. Her cats came first—and that meant their training took precedence over other people's entertainment.

Her devotion to those cats extended outside the ring as well. She never allowed anybody else to take care of her animals, personally handling all their feeding and cleaning and care. If one of her cats got sick, she would stay with him, sleeping just outside his cage and tending to him at all hours of the night, for as long as it took for him to recover.

"Why, half the training is caring for them," she would say.

Mabel was one of those people who are much better with animals than they are with people. The affection she lavished on those tigers didn't extend to the humans around her, and while she never spoke a harsh word to her cats, she was a loner, and her abrupt manner with people put them off. This didn't help her already rocky relationships with many of her colleagues, who had a lot of ego invested in believing that taming lions and tigers was a macho man's job. The fact that Mabel, a little old lady, was able to train her cats with affection and love instead of with threats and violence made the job look too easy.

One fateful day, a call came down from the office. "Sorry, Mabel, but we have to let you go. The insurance company won't let you work. You're just getting too advanced in years."

Mabel may have been elderly, but there was far more risk in acts that used the whip, the chair, and the gun. Mabel's cats loved her, and you never felt that she was in special danger because of her age or size when you were watching her in the ring. Mabel had her own theory: there had been rumors, spread by her jealous competitors, that she wanted to die in the arena, and she believed that this gossip had gotten back to the insurance company. "It's not true," she insisted. "Why would I put that on my lovely cats?"

But the owner had made up his mind, and Mabel's fate was sealed. She asked one last question: "What will happen to my babies?"

Nobody had ever worked with her cats before, and it wasn't clear that they would transfer to another trainer without problems. The owner hesitated. "We'll have to give them to Stroker to break, I guess. We have too much money in them to let them sit idle."

Stroker was known as a great arena trainer, and it was true: his performances were spectacular, and always popular with the public. What the public didn't know was that he would do anything necessary to get his cats to obey him. His methods were brutal and unforgiving.

Stroker had unknowingly provided my own introduction to "fear training" on one of my early visits to Jungleland. Exploring early on a Saturday morning, I'd found a large old barn standing in the middle of a clearing, far away from the public areas of the park. Inside, I saw a temporary steel arena, the kind set up at fairs, studios, and carnivals for a day or week.

Stroker stood in the middle of the ring holding a long pole. With him was a half-grown Bengal tiger. She was foaming at the mouth and breathing heavily. A thick chain was tied to a post outside the ring and ran though the bars to a collar around the cat's neck.

Each time he approached the cat, she would snarl and leap for him, and the chain would catch her entire body weight, cruelly snapping her back. And each time she went for him, Stroker would bring the pole down hard, cracking the cat across her body. Large welts appeared on her sleek fur. Stroker was yelling at the tiger in German the whole time. I later found out that he had been attacked years before by a big cat who had knocked him headfirst into one of the heavy steel pedestals in the ring, smashing his head and causing permanent hearing loss. He refused to wear a hearing aid because of his ego, so everything he said was at top volume.

I recognized the tiger. A few big cats, lions and tigers, had recently arrived at the park from overseas. They were all half-grown and had come directly either from the wild or from zoos. In either case, they were petrified of their new surroundings. It was Stroker's job to "break them"—to break their spirit, and put the fear of mankind into their hearts so they would do whatever their trainer asked of them in the future.

The tiger tried over and over to attack the man who was provoking her, but she finally realized that it was useless. Exhausted and demoralized, with the raised weals on her sides and back angry and bleeding, the cat finally started to back away from the pole. When he could no longer antagonize her, Stroker knew he had won. He had a veterinarian tranquilize her and remove the chain.

He then set barrels around the arena. When the effects of the tranquilizer wore off, the cat ran from Stroker. To get away from him and the threat of his violence, she had to jump the barrels. He used the whip and pole to guide her and keep her on the move.

The arena was round, so Stroker couldn't be cornered. A chair was kept nearby, in case the cat decided to go for him. The four legs of a chair would confuse her until the pole or whip—or if necessary, the gun—could come into play.

This "breaking of the spirit" was the fate awaiting Mabel's lovingly trained tigers, and it was a future that Mabel couldn't face. The idea of her beloved cats in the hands of this monster was too much, but there was nothing she could do. That night, she went home, wrote a note to a friend, put a plastic bag over her head, and died in the most honorable way she could.

I will certainly never forget her, and I have heard other trainers who were young at that time say the same thing. She was the first woman I ever saw working with big cats in an arena, and her non-violent, affectionate technique was an inspiration for what came to be my own philosophy of animal training, one that I would expand into movie studio work. I didn't necessarily use her methods, but I was inspired by them. Eventually I would prove that my technique allowed me to do everything that fear training did, and more.

7

 When Zamba came into my life, I was beginning to refine the idea of affection training. I decided that I would use this new system to raise him.

My animal training peers had told me that I was flirting with danger, and that I would surely be mauled or killed when he grew out of cubhood. But I had already seen (and experienced firsthand) the results of fear-based training, and I had no intention of raising a lion that way. Deep in my gut, and with every fiber of my being, I knew it was wrong.

Men have pitted their strength against animals since time began. In many cases, their success in that battle was key to their survival. But there has always been a dark underbelly to that contest: man's desire to cause pain and death in animals, and to witness acts of cruelty against them.

Think, for instance, of the Roman gladiators. In the Colosseum, an amphitheater that could seat more than fifty thousand spectators, animals were forced to battle other animals to entertain the crowds. The arena was designed with a maze of passageways beneath the stage floor, complete with temporary holding pens for the animals, and a hand-operated elevator to convey them to the arena.

To feed the public's appetite for spectacle, North Africa, Europe, Asia and other areas were systematically stripped of their exotic animals. Many died as a result of the way they were captured; others suffered the long, arduous journey back to Rome, only to be killed by another animal in the ring. Unspeakable combinations of animals were thrown together to fight to the death and please the crowds—lions were put with bulls, tigers with bears. It was a tremendous success.

The emperor Nero introduced humans into the "sport." It is said that the emperor, witnessing a small carnival performance, was delighted to see the enthusiastic spectator reaction when a performer was attacked by one of the animals. Slaves, or those who opposed Nero politically, were brought to the arena and thrown to the carnivores—leopards, hyenas, tigers, and lions—to be killed, and in some cases eaten. They would tie elephants to each of a man's limbs, and then beat the elephants so they'd move, ripping the person to pieces. The nearby Circus Maximus became a proving ground for up-and-coming gladiators, men who sought to distinguish themselves in the eyes of the emperor and to win his favor by fighting men or animals.

In a way, I feel that the circus arena of today is but a smaller version of the Colosseum. It is still a demonstration of the contest between man and animal. Of course, nobody goes to the circus to see animals kill one another, or to see them kill a man.

Or do they?

I have spent much time talking to people who frequent circuses, and many will admit that they watch the arena not just to see the skills of the trainer and the beauty of the great beasts performing, but in the hope that there will be an attack.

You were quite a bit more likely to see an animal attack a human in the days before nonviolent training methods became the norm. It's no secret: frightened, abused animals are violent animals. So the situation created by the prevalence of fear training in the industry was dangerous, not only for the animals, but also for the trainers.

Because the conditions were so treacherous, many of the trainers drank just to get the courage to enter the arena. One well-known trainer had three glasses of booze lined up just out of sight of the public. He downed one just before he went into the ring, another halfway through just before his big number, and finally a third at the end—his reward for making it, I guess.

Many of the trainers I met during that time were maimed, losing fingers, hands, even arms. We heard about new and serious injuries—even deaths—every month. It always amazed me to see how proud the trainers were of their injuries. They were ready, even anxious, to show anyone who asked their claw marks and bites.

"Ya see this one?" asked Bruno, a star arena professional who called himself Catman in the ring. A large man with bulging biceps and shaved head, he rolled up his pants to reveal a huge hole where a fang had entered his calf, ripping out most of the tendons and muscle.

"That big Siberian over there." He pointed. "Ruby's her name. She's the one who got me. Just that quick she was, and she had me." I noticed a number of old scars on his arms and a massive one showing through his sparse arena costume that arched clear across his back. He continued, "But now that I'm back, I'll show her who's boss." Then he added, "Even if it means doing her in."

I saw many trainers like Bruno during the forty years that I worked in the motion picture and television industry. I personally believe a good trainer shouldn't have any bites or claw marks. I've been asked over the years to show my scars as though they were badges of honor, and I'm proud to say I have only a few—and most of them are from climbing through barbed wire ranch fences. Bruno would have called me a coward.

But I believe in the yin and yang of life, that all things have an equal opposite, like love and fear. I believe that these emotions are merely different sides of the same energy. It was my belief that I could use positive energy, or love, to overcome any negative energy—fear or hate. Every living being needs love, and it is through love that we learn. All the existing training systems used fear, but it didn't make sense to me. I recognized immediately that the single most important element was to establish a form of communication between the human and the animal. How could any real communication be possible between two parties when one was made to be afraid of the other?

I felt sure that a gentle, emotion-based path was the key to reaching the inner world of an animal. I knew the animal would understand and accept the affection I gave it, and it had always been my experience that a desire to please goes hand and hand with affection. Just because an animal is physically stronger than a human, and is accustomed to using that strength to achieve its desires, didn't mean that it couldn't be taught a different way.

I also believed then, as I do now, that effective communication between man and animals is the key to a better relationship with the whole earth. If you could *truly* get in touch with all that is awesome and powerful about nature through a relationship with an animal, would you still pollute the environment? Of course you wouldn't. My hope was that some day my affection-based system would become the universal language between man and animal.

Determining how to do this was a little more complicated. How *does* one say no to an animal as big and dangerous as a lion without physically instilling fear? Could there be respect without needing to resort to violence?

According to my philosophy, if there was to be a reprimand, it would have to be an *emotional* one and not a physical one. If there is love between two individuals, then the greatest pain is to emotionally "hurt," or upset, the other. Anyone who has ever raised a child knows that communicating disappointment is a far more effective way of exercising discipline than any threat or coercion could ever be. Because the child cares about your opinion of him, your disappointment motivates him to do better the next time.

To train animals without using physical pain, I would have to establish a loving relationship with that animal, and then find a way to cause emotional "pain" to deliver a reprimand.

In itself, this is a dangerous game. If the animal doesn't have affection for you, its feelings will not be hurt by a reprimand. If you hurt the animal's feelings in the wrong way, or too acutely, or if your timing is off, you run the risk of confusing the animal, and being misunderstood. Any misunderstanding with a large, potentially dangerous animal is to be avoided, especially since accidentally causing anger can be a life-threatening situation.

As I had learned in my early days at Jungleland, many of the people who got into animal training had difficulty in showing any kindness or love to their animals. Most of them were men, and the kind of men who felt that loving an animal and showing it affection would make them sissies. Luckily I had no such hang-ups. Affection came easily to me as soon as I was in the presence of an animal, and I grew increasingly convinced, after years of studying other training procedures, that affection and emotional control could be the basis for an extremely effective and cruelty-free animal training system.

Once you have an emotional bond with an animal, it's a very powerful tie, and not one to be abused or treated lightly. I learned this lesson once, the hard way. It was late in Zamba's life, after we had happily been working together for many years, and I made a terrible and tragic mistake, one that violated his trust. The director of the movie we were working on needed him to "die" on camera. The scene was to be a close-up. How do you train a lion to convincingly act a death scene? I knew of only one way to hurt his feelings. So I yelled at him. "What are you doing, you dumb animal? I can't believe you did that! Bad lion! Stupid Zamba!"

I had never spoken to him in that way. He had spent his entire life knowing that I supported and loved him, even if he made a mistake—and then, all at once, I yanked the carpet out from underneath him. The director got his shot, all right. Zamba rolled over in bewilderment and pain, bowled over by the emotional weight of my anger. I knew instantly that I'd crossed a line that shouldn't be crossed, and tears sprang to my eyes. I got to my knees and buried my face in his mane, begging forgiveness, but he wouldn't make eye contact with me. And he was off-color for weeks, listless and barely eating although I was tempting him with his favorite treats, and showing none of his usual enthusiasm for life. I feel sick even writing about it now, and can assure you that I never did anything of the sort again.

At the beginning, I called my system the EBC (emotional behavior concept). As time went by, it became known by the media as affection training. I always worried a little about the consequences of such a name. While it was true that the program required affection on both sides, many people assumed that affection was the *only* thing you needed to train an animal. Of course, that's preposterous. Without emotional discipline and a great deal of knowledge, pure love produces a spoiled animal, one that has the potential for behavior even more dangerous than the behavior it might exhibit in the wild. Ultimately, though, the name stuck, and I've gotten used to it.

The philosophy behind affection training is simple, and it's always a two-way street. The key elements, for both human and animal, are:

LOVE: a total commitment to each other.
PATIENCE: an infinite amount.
UNDERSTANDING: so we know each other's strengths and weaknesses.
RESPECT: so we don't take advantage of each other.

I had been honing the philosophy for years. With these elements in the right combination and proper balance, I was sure I could raise a happy, healthy, loving, and secure animal who would be a joy to work with.

And as soon as I met him, I knew that Zamba would be the animal to prove my theory.

8

The philosophy behind affection training may have been simple, but its implementation was not. As committed as I was to training without violence, affection training was an idea before its time, and I took a lot of flak from my competitors, who often told the studios that my methods were too dangerous.

For affection training to work, the animal had to begin when it was very young—six weeks was ideal. When you bring an animal up with affection training, you become that animal's mother and father. Unlike "regular" methods, the training is not made up of small lessons but takes place twenty-four hours a day, seven days a week.

That's why I had Brini and Jack bring Zamba to my ranch in the Santa Monica mountains. I felt that it was important for him to experience as natural a setting as possible and grow within an environment suited to his way of life. Thankfully, the ranch was everything he could ever want. Its wide-open spaces gave him ample room to roam as well the opportunity to be involved with the staff and a vast array of exotic animals. It allowed him the right balance of freedom and restrictions.

I wanted to raise Zamba as a member of my own family. To train him the way that I wanted to, I had to become his everything. I had to protect him and to care for all his needs. I needed to become his teacher, and I was looking forward to learning from him as well.

Most of the trainers I knew felt I was treading on dangerous ground.

"He's cute now, but when he matures, it's going to be a whole different story," they said. "His real nature will reveal itself and do you in. He won't be able to help it."

Perhaps, I thought, but I was determined to see it through.

As you might imagine, inviting a lion cub into your house means a significant change in your way of life—for both of you. I was happy to provide accommodations, but there were a couple of rules that Zamba had to follow.

Potty training was the first step. It was also one of the easiest. When I showed him the dirt-filled box he scratched a bit, and then anointed it, and it was settled. In all the time young Zamba lived with me—whether we were in a new house or a new country—he always used his box.

When he got older and outgrew the largest size, we had a very large "doggy" door built into the back door so he could do his business outside, by the beautiful pepper tree in our yard. He moved around with no restraints—an important step in his training. As he grew, we had to keep cutting the door bigger and bigger so his back wouldn't scrape the top. Once, on one of his "duty calls," he carried the screen door on his back into the yard! On one or two occasions when Zam was full-grown, he couldn't make it to the backyard in time. Both times, he used the house cat's box—it was amazing and very gratifying to see how accurate his aim was.

Like the other animals, Zamba used the pepper tree to sharpen his claws, but he also needed a place to do it inside. Every domestic cat owner has had the experience of spending a lot of money on a fancy cat post, only to find that kitty prefers the couch. I was worried about the same thing. I knew that whatever I introduced had to be compelling enough to entice him away from the objects in the house, different enough that it would attract him.

On a trip to the mountains, inspiration hit, and I brought back a large, heavy, strong-smelling cedar log. It stood some six feet tall and had a few thick limbs protruding from it. All the small branches were gone. I washed it down and thoroughly scrubbed off all the forest debris until the fresh underbark appeared. Upending it, I braced it into the floor in the corner of the room with heavy metal brackets. Voila—the biggest cat-scratching pole in the world!

I reasoned, and correctly so, that the smell separated it from the other objects, and revealed it as more than just another piece of furniture. The war was not yet won, though—it took the destruction of a few pieces of African art and a heavy canvas chair, and a lot of compliments before Zamba fully comprehended why the cedar log was there, but once he got the hang of it, he never strayed from it. It was also his favorite place to scratch an itch—and when he was done, he walked away smelling like a tree.

He was a perfect gentleman, and always kept his claws retracted unless he was sharpening them on his tree. About once every month I would look them over to see if they needed filing. Most of the big cats don't need any work on their claws: they do a very good job of keeping them filed by themselves. And that's a good thing, because most cats, domestic or exotic, don't like to have their paws and claws handled.

But occasionally big cats would get what we called a "lag" claw. This is when the tendons in the claw no longer support it, so it hangs down instead of retracting like the others. A lag claw is constantly getting caught on things, and would certainly wreak havoc on any bedding or the rugs in the house. And as you might imagine, a lag claw also has the potential of being very dangerous when the cat is playing with humans because he has no control over it. It could very easily snag skin or hook into your body.

So I was conscientious about taking care of Zamba's claws regularly, even though getting his pedicure was not a pleasant experience for him. It was important to get him used to having his paws and claws handled while he was still young. I didn't want to be doing it for the first time when he was an adult with a lag claw!

Like everything else with Zamba, he'd cooperate, but only if you did it his way. In this particular instance, that meant that he had to be lying down when you were cutting his nails. He wouldn't let me trim them if he was sitting or standing; I had to lie down so he could lie next to me and rest his head on my lap. Then, one by one, I would slide the skin back to reveal the claw. When he was a cub, I was able to use regular domestic cat claw trimmers, but as he grew, so did his claws. Eventually I had to use a massive pair of mechanic's dikes, like a pair of cutting pliers, to get the bulk of them. I did the precision work with the coarse side of a nail file. Each nail took a while because he didn't want me to use a big file—I don't think he liked the noise.

The biggest claw (and therefore the hardest to trim) was the dewclaw, the fifth toenail on a lion's foot. It sits high up on the leg, like a thumb. It's never sheathed, and it never touches the ground. To get at the dewclaw, I had to climb over him and sit with my back resting against his mane. Then I could pull his foot over my shoulder and get the job done.

Clipping Zamba's claws was thankless work: no matter how good a job I did, he would always go to his cedar tree and sharpen them.

I gave Zamba a bath once a week when he was a cub. Lions, like most cats, hate water, but I knew there would come times as an adult when we'd need to give him a bath. So I wanted to get him used to it early. I knew that we could make it fun, as long as I wasn't afraid of getting wet. I'd spray him (and me) with the hose, and we'd roll around and wrestle in the puddles, and eventually it became a special time together. Even as an adult, when the time came for his bath, he saw it as playtime.

He was beautiful after he'd had a bath, and it was a real joy to maintain Zamba's gorgeous mane and coat. He had an exceptionally spectacular mane. Huge, thick, and rich in texture, it reached from his head to the middle of his back and down under his body, covering his belly completely. The color was stunning, like spun gold, with light orange, yellow, brown, and ocher highlights and a fringe of black. His coat was the color of harvested straw, tawny with a tinge of burnt orange, and a thick burst of black hair tipped his tail.

I groomed him every day, using a variety of brushes and combs. I would always start at the least enjoyable spot. This made him sit still, knowing that the best part was yet to come. Like a little kid with curly hair, he didn't like it when I accidentally pulled his mane, and would complain loudly if the comb got stuck.

Zamba did a lot of commercial work, and one was for a well-known hair shampoo and conditioner. They wanted us to wash, condition, and curl his mane, just as if he were a woman. Of course, we had to use about seven bottles of the stuff, but we did it just as they'd asked. I can't pretend that he didn't look hysterical in the curlers, but the result was worth it—I'd never seen his mane as glorious as it was when we brushed it out.

Food is an important part of a growing lion's life, and it played a role in our training as well.

I never allowed Zamba to eat from a plate, but hand-fed him instead. I wanted him to feel my hand, and to know that it was under the slab of meat that he was eating for lunch. Hand feeding also reinforced to him that his only food came from my hand. Obviously, it was very important that he never snapped. In the early stages of training, I prevented this by overfeeding him a little, so that he was never in a hurry for his food and would take it gently. As I decreased the food he still responded the same way, gently, and after each meal he would lick my hand clean. I would often soak my hand in blood from the meat and allow him to lick it, so that he'd know the contours of my hand well, and never mistake a finger for a treat.

Sometimes he would wait quietly at the table while we ate dinner, sitting quite still by my chair, waiting for a sign that a small morsel was coming his way. It was one thing when Shaka, our Rhodesian Ridgeback, waited for a tidbit from the table, but when Zamba sat, his head was as high as mine. He watched every bite. Have you ever seen a lion drool? I had to put a bath towel down on the floor.

I know that a lot of people think that an animal has no place in the dining room, but I never considered his presence a problem; it was an honor to share a meal with him, as it is to share a meal with any close friend. I would mix a bit of meat in the stew sauce or combine cottage cheese with ice cream, and he would just sit and drool until his treat came.

Scraps from the dinner table don't sustain a growing lion, though—our meat bills were staggering. In a week, Zamba would eat about sixty pounds of meat—when he was growing, he could put away twelve or fifteen pounds a *day*. A nutritionist analyzed Zamba's diet as he matured, adapting the amount and composition.

Later, when he was full-grown, I would undertake quite a radical experiment with Zamba's diet: vegetarianism. I have always believed that there is a correlation between eating meat and having a violent nature. It's always baffled me why humans are carnivorous. Carnivorous animals kill to eat, and yet we humans don't have the physical abilities to kill—no claws, no fangs. Some anthropologists believe that primitive humans started as vegetarians, foraging from the forest and growing food crops, but when they saw other animals eating flesh, they began to eat it as well. I have often wondered what change in our psyche happened when we started killing animals to eat.

If it was possible for a vegetarian to become a meat eater, could the reverse also be true? Could a meat eater become a vegetarian? And what effect would that have on a carnivore's behavior? I wanted to see if a lion could be conditioned to become a vegetarian, without stress or force. I also wanted to know if it was the taste of the meat the animal wanted, or if there was something in it that they really needed.

Once again, Zamba was a perfect candidate to test my theory. I called our veterinarian, and together with a top nutritionist, we came up with a menu that would give a carnivore a full and healthy diet without meat. The essential elements included eggs, milk, rice, pasta, beans, soy, meat flavoring, calcium extract, oatmeal, legumes, tomato sauce, and cocoa, blended with a wide variety of vegetables, vitamins, and mineral supplements. We didn't feel that it would be good for Zamba's system to have a drastic change in his diet right away, so to begin with, we added 70 percent organ meat. Our plan was to slowly reduce the amount of organ meat until there was none added to the meal. Our first batch of the new formula ended up as a ten-pound cake.

I decided to use two full-grown lions to test our cake—Zamba, who had been hand-fed since cubhood, and a second lion who was a zoo animal, who was not tame at all, but wasn't afraid of humans.

We waited two days after their last regular meal before starting the program to make sure they were really hungry.

Zamba sniffed at the cake, picked it up, and shook it a few times before he slowly proceeded to eat certain parts of it. He stopped a few times, smelled it, then continued eating. I noticed he would separate certain foods, eating only those he favored, so we learned what was appealing to him and what was not. If he left some food aside entirely, we'd take it out, as long as we felt it wasn't an essential part of his diet. We tried different combinations for a number of weeks, until we felt we had the right mix.

We started reducing the meat about 5 percent every other day. Within six weeks, the cake was meat-free, and yet he never hesitated to eat it. Finally we took away the meat flavoring. He hesitated a bit but continued to eat.

I looked for any signs of lack of interest. I didn't want him to feel he had to eat it to please me, although I wasn't really that worried about it; cats are particular, and I knew that if he really didn't want it, he'd have refused it altogether.

The other lion was a bit slower in his response. He sniffed and played with the first cake for a few minutes before eating any of it. He would also separate certain foods, and we exchanged those for others. Interestingly, the foods he discarded were not the same as the ones Zamba had turned his nose up at—apparently, it was a matter of individual taste! He eventually ate it all. After a relatively short period of time, about two months, the cake was accepted fully by both lions.

From this experiment we observed five important things. First, lions normally have a bad case of halitosis. They had little or none when on the vegetarian diet. Second, their skin and coats appeared fuller and cleaner. Ordinarily, when you run your hand down a lion's back, you will feel an oily substance on its skin, and your hand usually comes away dirty. The meatless diet seemed to alleviate that problem significantly. Third, I also saw a noticeable change in temperament. Zamba was less lazy, and more willing to do things. He had more energy and vigor than I'd ever seen. The wild lion seemed more docile, and had a good attitude. I concluded that meat seemed to make the lions more lethargic. Fourth, the other lion didn't bolt his new food (Zamba never did), but took it slowly, which had to be better for his digestion. Fifth, their overall physical appearance was better. Their bodies took on sleeker lines.

It was never my intention to continue this diet—lions eat meat, and I never go against nature when I can avoid it. It was just an experiment to see if lions could be made to eat a vegetarian diet—and so they can.

Some questions remained for me. Why are there so many meat eaters? Some people say that without the carnivores the other animals would multiply out of control. Maybe. I continue to have questions about the correlation between eating meat and violence. Since we must kill to eat meat, does this reflect our true nature? Or are we really going against that true nature, and encouraging violence in ourselves, by eating it? Would humans be killers today if we had not started to kill to eat meat? I wonder.

Zamba grew quickly, and I took him practically everywhere with me. When he was little, we'd keep him on a small dog collar with a leather lead. He grew out of that—into a large dog collar, and eventually a welded chain-link lead attached to the collar with a swivel that prevented the chain from twisting and choking him. We had the chain bronzed so it looked quite beautiful against his neck. Obviously it was metal, and sensitive to hot and cold, so we always made sure it was kept out of direct sun in the summertime, and on cold winter mornings, some unlucky passenger would usually end up sitting on it all the way to the studio, so it wouldn't chill our royal Zamba's neck!

He *loved* to ride in my station wagon. We learned when he was young that he couldn't ride in the front seat: it was just too dangerous. He'd want to "play" with the steering wheel, or he would want to be in my lap, or he'd suddenly jump up to lick my face. So I was firm about him riding in the back. The car was designed so you could eliminate the backseats if you were moving something very large, and we kept them that way all the time. I had custom heavy-rubberized flooring installed back there. It gave him traction and saved the car from damage when he sharpened his claws. He couldn't stand up, or even really turn around, so he'd rest his head on the back of the front seat, his body filling the backseat. Of course, I couldn't see out the rearview, so I got very good at driving using only my side mirrors.

If the window was rolled down, he would stick his head out to catch the breeze. I can tell you that many a passerby was startled by the sight of this massive lion's head sticking out of the rear window! Sometimes it was pure comedy. People would trip getting up on the curb, or ride their bicycles into parked cars. It had the potential to be quite a dangerous situation! The scariest thing for me was when drivers would pull up alongside of me, going sixty on the freeway, trying to show their kids the "pussycat." I was always terrified that the car in front of them would stop short.

During the filming of the movie *Fluffy* in 1964, the script called for Zamba and Tony Randall to go for a ride in a convertible. To get the shot, they pulled off the studio lot and into real traffic, next to a car containing a yippy little dog who had been going crazy in the backseat of the car, barking at everything that went past and throwing himself around. I will never forget the look on that little dog's face when he got a load of Zamba. It certainly shut him up.

When we were on the road, Zamba was always meticulous about not using the car as a litter box. If he had to go, he'd use a nearby lawn. We carried a really super-duper pooper-scooper, and sometimes were able to catch it before it hit the ground. To Zamba, it was one of the baffling things humans did; I'm sure he wondered what in the world I was doing back there.

Occasionally we would go to the local drive-in movie theater. After all, we couldn't find a babysitter for a lion! Luckily, he loved going to the movies, especially to Westerns. The owner let us in free, although once a girl at the ticket booth wanted to charge us extra for him. A sleepy yawn from Zamba that displayed his rather large teeth quieted her down. We had to keep the windows rolled down most of the time as his breath would quickly fog them up, making it impossible to see the action on screen. Down in front!

9

 As I have said, Zamba's training was pretty much constant. Every moment we spent together was an opportunity to teach him something new about living in the human world.

Every domestic cat owner knows how hard it is to keep delicate knickknacks out of tail's reach. Imagine what it's like living with a cat who weighs five hundred pounds! Anything delicate on a table was fair game—with a bump of his rear or a swish of his tail, Zamba could smash my favorite things to smithereens without even noticing.

So one of the greatest challenges I faced when I invited Zamba to share my home was teaching him not to accidentally break things. Because I couldn't always be present when he put himself in a position where something could be broken, teaching him to be careful took more time and effort than all the other behaviors together.

Traditional commands weren't effective if the behavior wasn't deliberate. It didn't work to tell him no when he was about to knock over a statue by swishing his tail across the coffee table, because he had no idea what I wanted.

It was just turning into a serious problem when I had an idea. I completely rearranged a part of the house by taking away any breakable items and replacing them with "fake" ones. An empty pickle jar stood in for a piece of statuary. A tin cup filled with stones and fake flowers replaced a crystal vase filled with the real thing. It was a big job. We put the fake pieces in places we knew he would probably knock them over, and we picked items that made a noise when falling because he always reacted if the object he knocked over made a loud noise, and I thought this would make him understand the problem more readily.

It was like going to school, so I called it "the classroom." When Zamba was there, I was there to correct him. I tried to make it as much like a real domestic setting as possible, and spent as much time there with him as I could, eating many of my meals and living there as much as possible.

In the classroom, I discovered that most of the damage came from his tail. He didn't seem to know that it belonged to him! He'd whip his tail and send something crashing to the floor, and look back in surprise to see what had caused the commotion. And of course, swishing his tail was natural. We had to find some way to teach him that his tail was his, and that he was responsible for it.

Since just saying no didn't work, I got a long, thin, flexible reed. I tried it on myself, and was satisfied that it caused no pain. When Zamba hit something, I would nip the tip of his tail with the reed as a reminder, and at the same time, in a deep baritone voice, say, "NO!"

It took a few days before he related to it. There were times when I had to set him up, by calling him between two tables filled with fake knock-me-downs. And there were times when he knocked something over, and I couldn't correct him in time. As the object crashed to the floor, he'd look over at me like a spoiled kid, with a don't-you-care? look. But ultimately he wanted to please me, and as time passed, the word "no" was enough to remind him to mind his tail before it did any damage. In a week or two, I was able to lay the reed aside.

Learning the word "no" was really the beginning of Zamba's education. In fact, it's usually the first, and quite possibly the most important, step in training any animal.

When you're relying on a command to control an animal, it's essential that it understands and responds to "no!" When it hears that word, it has to stop in its tracks and wait for the next command before proceeding, or you can get into a dangerous situation. "No!" has to be the voice of God Almighty for that animal.

This is for their own protection, more than anything. It's the same thing with children. If you see your son or daughter heading off the sidewalk into a crowded intersection, you need to be able to yell, "NO!" and have the child stop in his tracks. You can (and should) explain later about looking both ways before you cross the street, and the importance of waiting for the light, but what you need at that immediate moment is obedience, or you're going to be in big trouble.

So it was with Zamba. Especially at the beginning, it's important that the animal relate the act to the word, so the timing of the command was crucial. It was also very important for me, and everyone else participating in his training, to be consistent. "STOP IT!" or "DON'T!" were no good—it had to be "NO!" So we worked together until he knew that when I said, "No"—whether it was shouted or simply stated in a soft, firm manner—he was to stop whatever he was doing immediately.

At the beginning, we used reprimands like the reed to teach him "no," but he was a quick study, and there wasn't much need to use them for very long. And once he'd gotten something, he knew it, so except for the occasional refresher, we could move on.

And of course, showing appreciation is also a necessary part of the training. In the same way that "bad" behavior was accompanied by reprimands, "good" behavior was always followed with lavish compliments.

This may sound similar to how domestic dogs and cats are trained—and perhaps it is. There is, however, a unique and very important distinction between the two. Everything is significantly more dangerous when you're training an exotic. You cannot get a lion to stop eating a chunk of meat, or to stop breeding with his mate, unless your control is absolute. And you should never use this control in a frivolous manner. This trust is both a special gift and a necessity that can save lives or prevent an emergency.

I took special care with certain other aspects of his training, from the time he was a cub. Of course, it was important that Zamba respect and like humans, but because he would be living and working with other animals, it was also important to me that he learn to live cooperatively with them. Over the years I'd always found that lions had a superior, holier-than-thou attitude toward the rest of the animal kingdom, which might explain why they have been dubbed "King of the Beasts."

I felt that if Zamba was brought up with animals of different species, he would grow to accept them. So, when he was a cub, I introduced him to a group of very young friends: Sabu, a Bengal tiger; Rough, a Canadian black bear; Jeri, a chimpanzee; and Onyx, an African leopard.

Zamba lived in the house, and his friends lived in the animal nursery on the property. It would have been a serious mistake to try to raise them all in the house on a full-time basis. When you raise more than one animal at a time in the same environment, two things happen: jealousy and bonding, both of which can stand in the way of effective training.

Jealousy can create a very dangerous situation—either between the person and the animal, or between the two animals. It's easy not to notice jealousy when animals are young, because any skirmishes between them are easy to stop, but as they get older, and other factors come into play, jealousy becomes more dangerous, especially in a male.

While bonding is a worthy objective, it also has drawbacks. Exotics are fiercely loyal, and that means that their love is usually concentrated on just one very special person or animal. It was important to make sure that I was the object of Zamba's affection, not one of the other animals. Often, if you give an exotic another animal to befriend and live with because it's "lonely," you will find it doesn't need you, and that you have to compete with its playmate for its love. This isn't to say that it shouldn't have other close friends, but *you* must be the truly special one in its life, or the training relationship won't work.

So Zamba's friends stayed in the nursery, cared for by a staff of wonderful people, and his get-togethers with them were limited to weekends, which usually worked into a "sleepover" in the house. My bed would be covered in a pile of sleepy-eyed babies, all stripes and spots. The animals had a blast, and it was good fun for me as well. It was not, however, a good way to get a decent night's sleep. Someone would wake up in the middle of the night, wanting food. Someone would fall off the bed and need help getting back up. Someone would fall asleep on someone else's head, and the one on the bottom would protest. Every single one of them would wake up as soon as the sun was up, and that was when playtime started. So if you wanted rest, you were better off on the couch.

With his buddies, Zamba took the lead role right away. It wasn't size, although he was bigger than they. It might have had to do with the fact that he lived in the house, or it could just have been that he was a lion. Whatever it was, he was never cruel or arrogant, but it was clear to everyone that he was the boss.

From the very beginning, Zamba was incredibly friendly to people and to animals. He had no preference as to size or shape, two-legged or four. He would sidle up to you in the total belief that you were going to be his friend. And God knows, there is nothing cuter than a lion cub. Everybody wanted to cuddle him, and it was a struggle to keep him from getting spoiled. A real test of his discipline was for him to follow a command, even if it meant leaving an affectionate snuggle. I will confess that I often used this situation to reassure myself of his obedience.

Because he was so friendly, he got confused when people were scared of him. Our neighbor called the police when she thought Zamba was "killing" her little boy. All he was doing was licking the ice cream off his face!

He was a playful cub, so much fun to play with that it was easy to get wrapped up in playing with him, and to do nothing else. Luckily, he never lost that playful quality, even when he was full-grown. In one of his favorite games, he'd assume the I'm-asleep position, while peeking at you through his half-closed eyes. Then, without any notice, he would leap straight up, paws outstretched in an attempt to grab you and pull you down. If he was successful, he'd spend a few minutes licking your face—not quite realizing that his tongue was built to take meat off bone.

Zamba was polite to everyone, but he definitely had preferences. Over time, I could tell pretty much right off the bat whether he liked someone. And he was extremely sensitive—preternaturally so, I'd say. Once, as an experiment, I asked someone I knew he didn't like to prepare his dinner. Zamba had no way of knowing who'd cut his meat, but he wouldn't eat that night until I'd had another handler replace the "tainted" meat with fresh.

As friendly and well-behaved as he was, there were definitely moments when Zamba's "lion" came out. For instance, he could be overprotective. One time, he scared a middle-aged woman half to death by roaring at her when she got too close to our car in the parking lot at the supermarket.

It was important to impress upon people that Zamba was a full-grown African lion—a wild animal, not a pet. A lion, no matter how docile, is still a lion, and a lion is always potentially dangerous, an animal first. People would see us on the set together, and they'd see how he comfortable and loving he was with me. But that didn't mean they could come over and pet him as if he were my poodle. (I don't even think you should march up to a dog you don't know and pet him without his handler's permission, but that's another story.) I was always astonished by how presumptuous people were, and would sometimes surreptitiously give Zamba his cue to snarl when someone was failing to show the proper respect. There was no malice behind the snarl—he was just doing what he was told. But that black lip curling back to reveal those enormous fangs always had a sobering effect on our unwanted company. They didn't need to know that they could have safely put their hands right in his mouth.

We always asked people not to approach Zamba directly from the front—a dangerous place to be if something went wrong. I would hold him and stand next to his head, and the person could come up behind me and pet him or have a picture taken, or whatever. If theirs was to be an ongoing relationship, I'd have them work their way around to the front of him so he could smell and bump them himself.

You have to be careful where you touch a big cat, and how you pet it. It feels good to be petted, for both humans and animals, but, as with humans, "heavy petting" can trigger a sexual response in an animal. If you have a cat in your house, you know that when you stroke its back, it will press up into your hand with its tail lifted. This is a sexual response. Domestics will often whip around and grab your hand with their claws extended, holding tight, and in some cases, they'll even draw blood.

Certain exotic cats will have a similar response, but on a much more dangerous scale. Big cats can flop down, roll over, and demand stimulation that you may not want to give. Wrestling in play also has this potential; the cat may get "turned on" due to the close body contact, and can react by becoming aggressive, and refusing to let you go, using claws and fangs.

I learned this one the hard way. During a stunt, I wrestled with a lion, and our encounter went past the point of no return for him. He became extremely possessive, claws out, snarling to let me know that I was his, and I couldn't move an inch. I yelled to my men to get a sheet of plywood. Thankfully, we were on the studio lot, where construction supplies are plentiful. They brought one, about four feet by eight, and edged the plywood sheet between the lion and me. He was too intent to notice that I was slowly being separated from him. When the board was in place I carefully crawled out from underneath, and once I was on the other side, the lion reverted immediately back to his happy, normal self, as if nothing unusual had happened. It was always important to be mindful of these things when you were playing and working with any lion.

And sometimes, although rarely, Zamba was just unruly. One

incident stands out in my mind. When he was almost full-grown, I was invited to dinner by a couple who had heard me give a lecture on "Exotic Animals in the Home." They asked me to bring Zamba. They had given me a fair amount of money for animal programs in need, and I thought it would be a good experience for Zamba, so off we went.

For some reason, Zamba's behavior was appalling that evening. Everything that could have gone wrong, did. As soon as we got there, he spotted the lady's artificial rabbit skin coat—and attacked it, giving it quite a thrashing. When I finally got it away from him, it was ripped and torn to pieces. Personally, I didn't mind, but once he had finished "killing the rabbit," he proceeded to pee on the furniture! As dinner was served, he gave an explosive sneeze and a shake, thoroughly spraying the meal with lion snot. And during dinner, he wandered off into the kitchen and helped himself to a drink from the punch bowl.

Although our hosts were gracious, I couldn't wait to get him out of there, and I said our good-byes with a palpable sense of relief. Unfortunately, Zamba wasn't through. On the way out, he pinned their Great Dane to the floor and wouldn't let him up. They thought he was going to kill their pet! Needless to say, we weren't asked back.

More often, however, it was humans who screwed up. On one shoot, for instance, Zamba was hired to "attack" a policeman. We practiced the move with a stuntman in costume, and everything went beautifully. The stuntman went off to have his makeup touched up while they were setting up the shot for real, and my assistant accidentally gave a cue. Zamba cooperatively went for the nearest policeman—a watchman who just happened to be guarding the gate to the set. Poor guy! He almost had a heart attack.

10

 As a cub, Zamba slept in my bed most of the time. Many people were genuinely shocked to discover that I shared my bed with an African lion, and more people than I can even count asked me how someone of sound mind could do such a thing. I never worried about it. I believe that when you have devoted your life to something, it is important to see it through, no matter what comes. Zamba was sharing my life, and that meant he shared my bed.

Being able to do this at all was a real gift for me. Believe it or not, I started out life allergic to cats. In fact, it was during my job at Hollywood Aquarium that I overcame the first serious obstacle standing between me and a career working with exotic animals: myself.

Mr. Lloyd had never carried puppies or kittens in the store. "They eat too much," he said. But one day as I entered the shop, I noticed four kittens in the window.

"An old friend asked me to sell them for her. I told her I would try if she paid for the food."

After about an hour, I started to sneeze violently. Over the course of the afternoon, the sneezing grew progressively worse and was accompanied by a cough.

Mr. Lloyd sent me home so I wouldn't infect him or the customers with whatever I was coming down with. (He didn't hesitate to remind me that he wouldn't pay me if I wasn't working.)

I petted the kittens on the way out, and went into a sneezing spasm so intense I couldn't breathe at all. Once I was outside, it subsided a little. I leaned against a parked car, bent over double, and tried to catch my breath without throwing up. But by the time I got home, my mystery cold had essentially disappeared.

I realized that I was allergic to the kittens.

Unbelievable. Here I was, on my way to being the world's best animal man, one who could work with any animal, no matter how fierce—lions, tigers, leopards, and all the rest—and I was allergic to kitty cats?! Ridiculous. I just wasn't going to let something like this stop me from realizing my dream. So the next morning, I went to the library at school and read up on allergies. Most interesting. I read that they were manifestations of the body's sensitivity to some substance, like wool or milk or any number of things. But then I came upon something that caught my eye, an article on a metaphysical approach to disease and treatment, looking at physical problems as reactions to emotional unease. According to the article, in some cases, people had successfully used their minds to heal their physical problems.

I wondered. Could my allergies be caused by an emotional problem? Could I heal my body through sheer willpower? At a base level, this made sense to me. If the mind allowed the pain, it could allow the healing. If it caused the illness, it could also cure it. I knew what I was going to do.

"Mr. Lloyd, may I take the kittens home this weekend?"

"Why?"

"Well, they're fun and I think they can help me get over my allergy."

"These little farts caused your problem. How are they going to help you get over it?" he barked.

I didn't exactly feel like explaining my theory of metaphysical healing to Mr. Lloyd.

"Ach! Go ahead, take them. But you pay for their food!" he yelled after me.

"Yes, sir," I said.

The sneezing and headaches started the minute I picked them up. By the time I got home I was wheezing so badly I could barely get enough breath to speak. I couldn't eat my dinner. My mother, thinking I had come down with a cold, put me in bed.

I slept with the kittens all night. By the following day, I felt much weaker and looked quite pale. The kittens had slept up around my face the whole night, so their fur was all over the pillow. My mom wanted to take me to see the doctor, but I told her it was just a cold. It took hours to convince her I would rest and not go over my limitations. I didn't tell her about my experiment.

I don't remember much about that week, which I spent sweating and shaking in my room alone. I didn't eat the whole time. But just when I thought I was going to have to abandon my project— and my dreams of lions and tigers—I slowly began to recover. My symptoms gradually abated, and it was a truly great day when I could cuddle the kittens close to my face and not suffer.

I had beaten the allergies! I had used my mind to control my body. My family even kept one of the kittens—and called him Sneezer. It was a tremendous eye-opener for me, and I was to use metaphysical healing many times again in my life.

So inviting Zamba into my bed was of major significance, and not only for the obvious reasons. Of course, if Zamba and I were going to be bedmates, we had to agree on a certain etiquette. He always got a complete bath. Of course, I had to feel confident about his litter training. He was also under strict instructions not to deliberately rip the bedsheets with his claws. It wasn't hard to train him to do these things because we started when he was so small, but I can't imagine how I would have done it when he was an adult.

Every night was almost the same. Zamba would patiently wait for me in the living room, curled up by the fire with Shaka. He'd go out to the pepper tree for a last-minute pee, and when he got back, I'd clean his feet with a damp towel and give him a complete inspection to remove any twigs caught in his mane or dirt on his coat from bumping the tree. When he'd passed my inspection, I gave him a signal, and he'd make one big leap onto the bed. Invariably, he'd be asleep as soon as his head hit the pillow. He was a sound sleeper, and usually slept the whole night without interruption.

Zamba had his own pillow, right next to mine. As he grew, his head still remained on the pillow, but his body angled down until finally he filled the bed. It took a special kind of wake-up call to figure out that Zamba had outgrown the bed: the whole thing literally fell apart in the middle of the night.

We needed a new bed. I asked Jerry, my carpenter friend, to assist me. By the weekend I had bought enough wood to build three normal king-sized beds. I measured Zamba as best I could. He kept flicking his tail, but I felt it didn't matter whether his tail was on the bed or not. I marked the wood at eight feet long and eight feet wide, then after thinking about it a moment, I went another six inches.

Jerry wanted to make sure that the bed was strong enough to support Zamba's weight, so we headed over to the hay barn where a heavy-duty scale hung. It was capable of holding up to one thousand pounds, but it was suspended from a tow chain. Jerry and I took a wooden platform that hay was usually stacked on and rigged it to the chain. Zamba didn't much care for the swinging but he was on it long enough for us to get a reading of more than five hundred pounds.

The finished bed would be too big to move in after it was built, so we set up our workshop in the bedroom. A local mattress company offered to make both the box spring and mattress for free in exchange for the publicity. It was okay by me as long as they made it extra firm! The mattress was much stronger than the ordinary kind. It was made of a cushion weave about a foot thick. When the pieces arrived, it took four people to get them into position.

The sheets and covers were next. I had contacted a linen wholesaler and described my needs, and they were happy to accommodate my unusual request. The sheets were triple the thickness of regular bedsheets, and woven so that they wouldn't rip. We secured them to each corner with a draw rope. I had two different sets of blankets: a lightweight set for summer, and a heavier one for winter. I should have forgotten about the heavier set. When you sleep with such a big animal, the whole room heats up, and you're usually quite nice and toasty, even without blankets.

So, two weeks later, Zamba and I had a new bed. It was huge! It looked like a giant slept there. Everyone at the ranch and everyone who'd participated in its creation gathered around to see Zamba's reaction. He eyed it uncertainly when he came into the bedroom, but jumped right up onto it when I gave the command. The mattress gave a little bit of a bounce. He circled a few times, sniffing every inch of his new bed, then settled down and immediately went to sleep. He loved it.

It was a big bed, but if I could do it over, it would have been even bigger. Zamba was an unrepentant bed hog. He always ended up in the middle of the bed, which didn't leave much room for me, and it was not unusual for me to wake up pinned underneath him when he rolled over in the middle of the night. "Get your butt off me and onto your own side," I'd say, pulling his hair. That usually worked. Zamba spent his dream life running over the Serengeti or chasing Shaka, and I can tell you that rapidly moving lion's paws will wake you up quickly.

Living and sleeping with Zamba from cubhood gave us a truly special rapport, and as he grew, there was real love and understanding between us. Just because he was a born killer and carnivore didn't mean that he couldn't be gentle and trusting. Living in such close quarters with Zamba allowed me into a place few others had been.

Zamba didn't sleep with me every night; it was also important for him to have private quarters of his own, in the compound out-side. One of the nights he was outside, I awoke to lightning illuminating my room. An electrical storm was raging over Southern California, and the deluge seemed like Noah's flood. But it wasn't the thunder that woke me; it was the not-so-distant roar of a lion. Zamba was afraid of lightning, and I knew as I crawled out of bed that I would have to spend the dura-tion of the storm holding his paw.

Just as an aside, I am awful at obeying my own rules. You shouldn't ever go into a lion's den without a backup person, let alone in the middle of the night when you know in advance that the lion is frightened. So, if you ever find yourself in similar cir-cumstances: do as I say, not as I did.

By the time I had walked the three hundred yards to the animal compound, I was completely drenched. I passed many of the other animals, all bedded down in their warm straw, under the thatched roofs. But not Zamba. When I arrived he was pacing back and forth between the indoor enclosure and the outside compound, growling his displeasure. The torrential rain had soaked his mane so that it hung down in a wet chunk across his face, down his shoulder, and across his back. Not so regal! Another flash of lightning lit the compound for an instant, and Zamba saw me. He roared in welcome and relief. I unlocked the door and went inside, baby-talking the whole time.

Imagine the biggest, wettest golden retriever in the world welcoming you home. Zamba came barreling through the mud, and I braced myself against the fence so I'd be able to support the weight of his affectionate embrace. He launched himself at me, grabbing my head in his wet paws, and I buried my head in my hat and jacket as Zamba's huge, rough tongue tried to find my face. After a little while, I was able to calm him down enough to fasten a chain around his soaked neck.

So there I was, in the middle of the night, with a cowardly African lion, wondering what I should do next. Zamba decided for me. As I opened the door, a flash of lightning sent him bolting down the muddy road, dragging me on my derriere behind him. I saw a huge shape taking form before us and prayed it wasn't a rock, but it was only the hut where the hay and straw for the livestock was stored. A gust of wind had blown the door open. Next thing I knew, we were inside.

Puffing hard from his ordeal, Zamba plopped down on a huge bed of straw, and I joined him; we collapsed like two kids who had raced each other until exhausted. The rain had washed most of the mud off us. When Zam realized he was out of harm's way, and owed me a debt of gratitude, I had to fend off more kisses, and suffered greatly when he settled his massive bulk across me, rendering me completely helpless. This was his way of showing appreciation.

I wiggled out from underneath him. Catching my breath, I ended up alongside him, with his forepaw dropped across my body. It didn't take long before his heavy breathing told me he was asleep, and although I struggled to keep awake, the sound of the rain lulled me, and I soon joined him in la-la land.

I woke a few hours later, with my face buried in his mane. The pungent smell of wet lion surrounded me. I slowly inched my way up until I was level with his huge head, face to face with him, and inches from his nose. His golden mane was definitely much thicker and softer here. His massive paw was entirely wrapped around my waist, and with every breath his dewclaw rubbed lightly against my skin.

Occasionally he'd hold a breath for what felt like forever, and then, when I was just giving up on hearing another one, he'd release it with a heavy sigh.

It was morning. A small bright beam of sunlight eased itself into our chamber, gleaming against the back of his ear. I could see all the veins there, a freeway with no traffic, and every time he exhaled, the light would slip off his ear and just graze the tip of one of his fangs, protruding slightly from his lip.

Unfortunately, as much as I was enjoying this blessed moment of communion, Zamba's hardcore lion's breath won out. It was time to get going.

I took a piece of hay and gently tickled the inside of Zamba's nose. His eyelids moved. I tickled his huge nostril again. It quivered and trembled, and finally he sneezed. I was hugely amused.

Lions are lazy, and it was going to take more than a sneeze to wake this one up, so I began tickling his nose again. Intent on my task, I failed to notice that one giant amber eye had blinked open and was fixed on me as I continued to drag the straw just along the outside of his nose. I have no idea how long he was watching me, but I will tell you that making contact with that enormous, staring eyeball gave me the shock of my life! I jumped halfway out of my skin, scaring Zamba, who also jumped.

Then it was open season—playtime had begun. He lumbered to his feet, out of his warm, comfortable bed, and his breath steamed in the chilly air like that of a fire-breathing dragon. I dived under a huge pile of straw just as he pounced. He ran around in circles, digging and searching for me. If I hadn't laughed, he wouldn't have found me. But the next thing I knew, he had me between his immense paws like a mouse, and started to lick my cheek. It takes only a few licks from a lion to draw blood, so I offered the tougher skin of my arm instead while I was wriggling free. I dusted myself off, pulled some straw from his mane, and we went out into the crisp morning air, heading back to the house.

This was certainly not the first time I had shared a bunk with Zamba, but this particular instance stands out in my mind as one of the happiest mornings of my life. It was a tremendous honor and privilege to know that this great animal, this killer of mammals, had taken me into his world and accepted me as one of his own. To curl up with a sleeping lion, to touch his fangs, to brush his mane, to tickle his nose—it was the realization of a lifelong dream, and it brought me one step closer to the infinite power of nature. I loved every minute of it, and I was always conscious that I had to live up to the awesome privilege I had been granted.

12

You don't see a whole lot of old lions in the wild—they may be the kings of the jungle, but they're also surprisingly vulnerable. The lucky ones have a life expectancy of about ten years. Of course, at the ranch, even when we could barely afford food for ourselves, we had the finest medical care available for the animals. But sometimes the best that money can buy isn't enough—it takes love and down-home ingenuity as well.

About once a month I would give Zamba's teeth a good scrubbing. It wasn't easy. He didn't mind it when you worked on his front teeth, and even his fangs, but to get to the back molars, I had to really get in there and pull his lips apart, and he hated that.

I was giving him his brushing one morning when he suddenly yanked his head away from me, knocking the toothbrush out of my hand, and sending cleaning solution all over the floor.

"Zam, what are you doing?" I snapped at him.

He moaned his apologies, but wouldn't let me continue. Something was up. I put away all the cleaning supplies, laid his head in my lap, brushed his mane for a bit, then slowly raised his lips and peered inside his mouth to see if I could find the source of the irritation. I saw right away what was causing the problem: his left fang was quite dark around the base, and the gums surrounding the tooth were swollen.

The next day our vet came out to take a look. I had brought Zamba out on the grass to lie under the shade of a big fig tree. It was cool and comfortable, and the minute he saw me sit down, he flopped down next to me. Doc arrived carrying his black bag, ready to do whatever was necessary.

"What seems to be the problem?" he asked, stroking Zamba's mane. Zam knew and accepted Doc as a friend, so he let him probe very carefully around the sore spot. "Is he eating his full meal every day?" he asked.

"Well, now that you mention it, no. Maybe half. I didn't think anything of it because sometimes when the weather's hot he goes off his food for a short time, but he's usually back on it within a week or so."

Zamba allowed Doc to look at the fang for some time. Each time he tapped it with his small metal instrument, Zam would jerk back in pain. After a few taps, he actually growled his discomfort. We also noticed an odor coming from his mouth that was different than his normal, terrible lion breath.

"Well, what do you think?" I asked.

"It's impacted. There's a lot of infection, and we need to get it cleared up right away. Either we have to get into the root cavity and get out all the pulp and treat the infection, or we have to extract the fang." Doc thought for a minute. "Cleaning all that infection out would at least save the fang. It may turn a darker color, but it should function okay."

"So what's the next step?" I asked.

Doc sat back, thinking about it. "That's the hard part. We'll have to put him under. I don't like to do that, because with a general anesthetic there's always a risk, a chance we could lose him. But he'd be in enormous pain without it, and too dangerous to work on."

I knew the risk, and I hated the idea of anesthetizing any animal unless it was under the most extreme circumstances. I had seen too many animals die.

I shook my head, "No. There's no way we're going to risk anything like that."

"I understand, Ralph, and it's your decision. But whatever you want to do, we should do it soon." Doc got up and gathered his paraphernalia. "Call me when you decide."

A quick handshake and he was gone, leaving me with one of the toughest decisions I would ever have to make.

Within a day, Zamba had gone off his food completely. He was grumpy, saliva dripped from his jaw, and I noticed that he never rested his head on the sore side. We couldn't go on like this. I called Doc back.

"Doc, can you come out? Bring your stuff. Be prepared for whatever, okay?" We had a complete operating room and facilities, so there would be no need to take Zamba into the hospital.

Zam and I were again waiting under his favorite tree when Doc arrived.

"What have you decided?" he asked.

"Doc, I just can't risk putting him out," I said, not able to look him in the eye. "So I've decided to clean it out myself—to give it a try, anyway. I think he'll let me. I really do."

Doc was thunderstruck. "WHAT! Are you crazy? The procedure is very delicate, and he'll eat you alive—friend or no friend. I can't let you do this, Ralph."

"Look, here's how I figure it," I said. I knew I needed his 100 percent cooperation, and kept talking as if the sound of my voice could convince him. "You know I've had quite a bit of training in the veterinary field."

In the early days of my career, there simply weren't very many vets who were capable of working with exotic animals. In most cases, it wasn't ignorance, but lack of opportunity: it was hard to get close enough to a fear-trained animal to examine and treat it. How can you physically examine an animal that's never been touched by a human in kindness? Add physical pain or sickness to that equation—disorienting experiences for any animal (or any human, for that matter)—and the situation could become dangerous very quickly.

Most zoo vets used tranquilizers when they needed to treat exotics, which made it even more dangerous. They'd have to correctly gauge the weight of the animal to get the dose correct, and then deal with an animal that was hallucinating, unpredictable, and suffering from the side effects of the tranquilizers, which often included diarrhea and a racing pulse—all of which made it impossible to really get a reading on the animal's health and to treat it properly. Too little of the drug, and the animal would become insane with pain and rage; too much, and death by overdose was a very real possibility.

Because of this shortage of capable doctors, I'd had to learn the basics to treat my own animals, and I had taken a number of courses in the hopes that I'd eventually be able to afford tuition for veterinary school. My business eventually took too much of my time for me to pursue that dream, but I picked up quite a bit of information, and it was to stand me in good stead over the years. At first I treated only minor cuts and bruises, but as I became more experienced (and as circumstances on the ranch dictated), I did bigger and bigger procedures. Our animals, of course, were affection trained, which means that you didn't need a tranquilizer to help them, much less to find out what was wrong in the first place.

Doc nodded.

"Zamba trusts me, Doc. I can't stand the risk of putting him under. Maybe I can pull it off. You tell me what needs to be done and I'll do everything you say."

"Right. Just like that? Ralph, this is crazy." Doc's face was the shade of a ruby red grapefruit. "You'll see. That whole area is ultra-sensitive. Just touching it will be so painful, he'll bite your finger off!"

"Doc, come on now. Zamba?"

Doc took a big gulp of air and was quiet a few moments. He looked at Zamba, then at me, and slowly nodded. "Okay, okay, I'll help. But as soon as I feel like this is getting too dangerous, I'm pulling the plug."

We spread a large sterile towel on the grass and placed Zamba's massive head in the middle of it. Doc laid out all his instruments.

"Here," he instructed. "Rub this on the gums gently."

He handed me a salve that Zamba didn't particularly like but allowed me to administer.

"It will numb the area a bit, and cut down on the pain. The tooth is impacted, with pus coming from the decayed root at the base." He held up a small instrument, made from a strong fiber, flexible and tough. It was just a little thicker than a horse's hair, and had a tiny scoop at the end of it. "Look at the tip of the fang. You see that small hole, right at the end? You have to take this pick and slowly, carefully, work it all the way down into the tooth to the root. As you go, scoop a little bit of the pus, draw it out, and go back for more."

The scoop was so small, I wondered if it could do the job. But I trusted Doc, so I washed my hands, sterilized the scoop, and rubbed Zamba's gum with more of the deadening cream. I was ready.

I laid Zamba's head on my lap and began to comb his mane. This was his favorite position, and he could relax this way for hours. Taking up the scoop, I gently slid back his lip and opened his mouth. I put the scoop into the small hole at the top of his fang, and slowly started to push. There was pus immediately. As I scooped, Zamba moaned off and on, and shifted his weight whenever I hit what Doc called a "hot spot." As I neared the base of the tooth, the pain seemed to intensify. Doc cautioned me that soon I would be hitting the nerves, and Zamba's pain would be excruciating.

"Be careful," he said.

The pus was running freely now, and Zam was coughing up the spume that was running down his throat. I placed heavy gauze around the tooth to catch as much as possible. The odor was horrendous. I spoke to Zam the whole time, telling him over and over how great a lion he was, and how impressed I was with his bravery. I could tell he was in terrible pain.

The fang was huge. For the better part of an hour I worked on that tooth, and Zamba let me do it. Once he stood up and shook his head, spraying pus, saliva, and blood all over Doc and me. We gave him a bowl of fresh water. He put his whole mouth in it and held it there. The bowl was instantly filled with the rot from his mouth, so we replaced it with another bowl. This one he emptied in a couple of gulps.

"Now for the hard part," said Doc. I noticed he was sweating as hard as I was.

I was bent over in a difficult position, and my back was killing me. As I dug deeper and deeper into the tooth, Zamba's body began to tense. Zamba and I were working in tandem. He was holding his breath, tightening throughout his entire body while I dug, and then, when I stopped, he'd let the breath out in a huge exhalation.

Doc was awed. "My God, this is amazing. Why is he letting you do this? He can't possibly know you're trying to help him."

I was just approaching the nerve center. The stench was unmistakable: putrid, rotted flesh. Zamba's eyes were closed.

"Wait a minute," said Doc.

He gave me a small syringe full of anesthetic. I inserted it into the hole at the tip of the fang and squeezed. The liquid running down the inside of the tooth seemed to cool the heat generated by the infection, and Zamba's body relaxed a bit.

"Let the anesthetic take effect—it'll be about five minutes."

Zamba, thinking it was all over, started to get up.

"Easy, boy, not just yet. Only a bit more to go."

Zamba eased back down and gave an exhausted sigh. It was clear that this had been a terrible ordeal for him. I combed his mane for a while, and then sponged his face and brow with a wet cloth.

"Okay, let's do it," said Doc, wiping his brow.

I steadied the scoop and moved it farther into the tooth than I had gotten before. I felt resistance, as if something was stopping it. I pushed gently, and suddenly the spongy thickness gave way, as if something had exploded.

Zamba let out a full-blown roar, knocking me over as he leaped to his feet. He was up coughing, wheezing, and shaking his head violently, and a huge volume of pus, mucus, blood, and saliva splattered over Doc and me. Doc disappeared over the nearest rise.

When I got my breath back, I ran to Zamba, who gave me his first-ever snarl. I answered back with a hug and lots of baby talk until he bumped against me and gave me a grudging grumble. Doc reappeared, and I helped him pick up his scattered equipment.

"You did it, son of a bitch, I don't believe it!"

"What happened?" I said.

"You broke through into the decayed root. It's taken the pressure off."

For the next half hour we squeezed antiseptic, penicillin, and streptomycin into the hole. I gave Zamba a couple of antibiotic shots in his butt. He'd gotten all his shots there since he was a cub, so they didn't bother him a bit.

For the next few weeks Doc and I watched him, treating when necessary. We filled the cavity, and Doc soldered a cap on the tip of the tooth to prevent anything from getting into it. At this point, the tooth had no feeling, so it wasn't too difficult a job. Over time, the tooth darkened a bit, but it never gave Zamba another moment's trouble.

Doc and I talked about our intervention many times after that day. First of all, it was sobering to realize that if Zamba had been in the wild, he'd be dead. A lion that can't hunt is a lion that doesn't eat, and that's a dead lion. And if starvation hadn't gotten him, the infection would have.

Then there were all the questions. Why did Zamba allow me to do what I did? Could he possibly have understood what I was doing? Did he allow me to "hurt" him because of his love for me, or is it possible that he knew exactly what was going on? Whatever the reason, my Zamba, God bless him, was back as good as new.

It was further evidence of the tremendous trust that affection training could foster in animals, and the awesome power this training had to facilitate communication between the species.

13

 Once trained, Zamba worked steadily, and I'm happy to report that when we were working, Zamba was always a real pro. We did lots of commercials, and any number of film and television appearances. You're probably wondering if you've seen him in anything. If you were watching TV or movies in the sixties and seventies, the answer is almost definitely yes.

He was the Dreyfus lion for years, for example. He did a Kit Kat commercial, and one for the movie *Around the World in Eighty Days*. He worked live as well: he was the lion for *Hallelujah Hollywood* at the MGM Grand Hotel, a massive stage tribute to classic Hollywood. There are many more examples—too many to remember or mention. It was Zambamania!

To be sure, the first few years with Zamba weren't easy, financially. Nobody believed that affection-trained animals were for real, and my competitors spread rumors that my animals were so well-behaved because they were tranquilized. But eventually the tables turned—the insurance companies began refusing to insure sets that used other people's animals because they were too dangerous.

That danger, I think, is the biggest difference between an animal that's affection trained and one that isn't. Let's say you're walking across the studio lot with a lion on a lead, and something happens—the lion steps on a "hot" electrical line, for instance, and gets a shock. Nine out of ten animals are going to turn on the nearest human in pain and outrage, which can be a very dangerous situation—not just for you, but for everyone on the set. But an affection-trained animal won't automatically "blame" you, and may even turn to you for comfort instead. It's a much safer scenario overall.

In Hollywood, it really is true that you are who you know. Stuntmen, property masters, producers—everyone who worked with us knew that my animals were gentle, trustworthy, and easy to work with, and the word-of-mouth really helped our business. Movie sets are dangerous enough without adding risk. Nobody wants to be scared of the wild animals on the set, and with me they didn't have to be.

We had an agreement with the studios that there would be no guns on the set with the animals. It was simply too dangerous; someone could easily misinterpret an animal's actions and overreact. What if the animal jumped up playfully, or someone didn't see me giving him a cue? Or if they made a mistake, which happened from time to time? My crew carried canisters of carbon dioxide, which would release smoke, a loud noise, and a puff of harmless gas—all we needed on the off chance that something went wrong, as I well knew from my early experience with Rex.

The very idea of someone doing violence to one of my animals in "self-protection" was enough to make me insane. Once, Zamba and I were called into Paramount to do a scene with Jerry Lewis.

The job was a piece of cake, a simple sight gag. All Zamba had to do was stand next to Jerry on the balcony of a set made to look like an enormous hotel. They got it in one take.

As Zamba and I were heading down the stairs, someone called out to Lewis, telling him how well the shot had gone. He said, "Well, I came prepared," and pulled a gun out of his inside pocket. "If anything had happened, I would have taken care of it." He blew away an imaginary wisp of smoke at the tip of the barrel.

My anger took my breath away. Anything could have happened! And then Zamba's beautiful life would have been snuffed out. I completely lost control, and got up in his face. "You mean you would have shot my lion if you thought he was going to do something? How can you judge? Who in the hell do you think you are?" I yelled, loud enough to stop everyone in earshot. "That pea shooter would have only made him mad enough to chew your ass."

Jerry had me thrown off the set, and got me barred from working at the studio for six months until he was finished with his movie and had moved on. I didn't care—there was other work for us. Nobody threatened my lion.

It's pretty rare that directors ask for an animal star by name, but soon everybody knew that Zamba was the crème de la crème. He was the go-to cat for close-ups, because of his extreme beauty, and he was the cat everyone turned to when they needed a lion to work with a movie star. In the same way that the high-wattage stars get the best trailers and the best makeup artists, they also got the best lion. Zamba was a star's star.

And he became well-known around Hollywood. I'd be working another job, and he'd be in the car with me. Ordinarily you needed a lot of paperwork to get animals on and off the studio lots, but everyone was a Zamba fan, and the guards would just wave us through.

We met a lot of people that way. I worked with Robert Mitchum on a picture called *Rampage.* The script had originally called for a jaguar, but everyone told the director you couldn't train a jaguar, so he had changed the cat to a leopard and called me to see if I had one. I did—but I also had a great jaguar called Raunchy who could do the role as it had been written. Raunchy and Zamba were buddies, so I'd often bring Zamba with me to the shoot to keep Raunchy company, and over the course of filming, he and Robert Mitchum became good friends.

It took a while, but affection training caught on, and I don't think I'm bragging when I say that we revolutionized the motion picture and television industry. Insurance companies heard about affection training and literally demanded that the studios use our animals because they were safer. Eventually our company, Africa U.S.A., became the world's largest exotic animal rental company. Our animals were used in movies, television, stage, and private performances. I have invoices in my files for more than thirty-five hundred jobs.

We had more than fifteen hundred animals, including elephants, tigers, lions, leopards, cheetahs, giraffes, various types of antelopes, camels, llamas, gorillas, orangutans, chimpanzees, rhinos, hippopotamuses, eagles, and ostriches. We also had an assortment of reptiles, which included alligators, pythons, cobras, rattlesnakes, and several varieties of insects, including praying mantises and tarantulas. We had a barnyard full of farm stock—cows and pigs and sheep—and of course, a number of dogs and cats.

We were the proud winners of a couple of dozen PATSY (Performing Animal Top Star of the Year) Awards, the "animal Oscars" given out by the American Humane Association. Zamba took home four or five of those as well.

We also trained a great number of the men and women who went on to do some of the best animal work in Hollywood. I never hired an experienced animal trainer, preferring to teach animal lovers the principles behind affection training. (To be honest, I hate the word "trainer," which has a whiff of the master-slave relationship for me. And you can forget about "tamer," for the same reason. I always call myself a behaviorist if I have to call myself anything.) I learned fairly early that it was easier to start from scratch. People who had experience "taming" animals found it too hard to abandon their bad old ways, and I'd find myself listening to them talking about "how you have to give a lion a crack every once in a while so he remembers who's boss." Not around my lions, thank you very much!

As much as Zamba worked, it was always a disappointment to me that the movie industry persisted in reinforcing stereotypes about exotic animals, especially the big cats. I rarely got calls for Zamba to show his loving and playful side—they always wanted him to be a killer. Even Clarence, our cross-eyed lion, who looked like the least threatening animal on earth, got roles that called for him to be part of a sight gag, instead of demonstrating any measure of affection in his personality. It's ironic how committed Hollywood was (and remains) to this vision of lions as savage beasts, especially considering that there's never been an animal who kills as viciously and indiscriminately as humans.

Every young starlet hopes for a break, and every older actress bemoans the lack of decent roles for older women. As it became clear what a real prize Zamba was, as both an actor and all-around good sport, I wondered if there would ever be a movie just for him, a star vehicle. If anyone deserved one, it was he, but Hollywood didn't seem ready to let an exotic animal have that big a role. Dogs and cats, sure—even a bear, like Gentle Ben—but not a lion.

14

Our animal family was growing and we needed room, so when Zamba was about two years old and two hundred pounds, I had found a larger ranch in the Santa Monica Hills and moved in. I kept the old place and split time between the two.

A lot of animals—and people—came to us because the word was out about our cruelty-free methods and our inability to say no to an animal in need. I became great friends with the actress Mae West and her sister by taking an extremely smart and talented (but badly spoiled) chimp called Coffee off their hands. And Coffee the prankster became an Elvis Presley favorite when he was out at the ranch. But that's another story for another time.

My team of helpers and behaviorists had come together from all parts of the country. Each person was a dedicated animal lover who had heard of my specialized work in the behavioral training of exotic animals. Although some had no professional knowledge of animals, they brought with them something far more important—love.

Some came and went due to outside obligations, but over time our little group had developed into a family. We cared for one another, worked together, and lived communally in the big house. It was a run-down, fifty-year-old Spanish hacienda. The house was nestled in a grove of giant eucalyptus trees at the very top of a mountain. On a clear day you could see the crystal-blue water of the Pacific Ocean some twenty-five miles away.

The house itself had a strange, and not entirely welcoming, feeling to it. The walls were cracked and the paint was peeling. It was built in a traditional U-shape around a courtyard with broken red brick tiles and a cracked stone water fountain at the center, toppled after years of neglect.

The foreboding atmosphere extended to the inside of the house. All of the sixteen rooms were strangely interlocked: there were doors in the backs of closets, and others behind mirrored walls. But practically the entire first floor was a single, open room, approximately fifty feet long and almost thirty feet wide, with an eighteen-foot ceiling. The feeling here was one of warmth and hospitality. At each end, staircases with oak banisters led up to the second floor. In the center of the room was an enormous walk-in fireplace made of flagstone and mortar brick; you could see and feel its warmth, no matter where you were in the room. The fireplace was our only source of heat, spreading warmth via vents throughout the house.

Outside, the property sloped gently down to a small valley. An ice-cold creek dodged its way through groves of oaks and patches of ironwood until it dropped off a rock cliff, cascading down the mountainside like a miniature waterfall.

A six-horse barn, complete with a hayloft and outside runs for the horses, dominated the valley. We built rows of chain-link cages to hold our exotic animals, as well as corrals with pipe fences for the hay-eating stock.

"No problem" was the team's unofficial slogan. We all shared the belief that by using a hands-on approach to working with wild animals, an approach based on love and respect rather than brutality, we could help to bring about a greater understanding of animals and an appreciation of their value to society. We felt sure that what we were doing would ultimately benefit mankind.

Ted, my headman and protégé, was a good-looking, muscular guy with a wonderful personality and a great love of nature. He shared my boundless optimism. Every day was a glorious event, and no matter how bad the circumstances might be, Ted shared my belief that with hard work, we could overcome it.

Don, a young teenager, had come to us after having spent many of his years as a runaway. After much negotiation with his parents (who did not want him) and the judge (who wanted to send him to juvenile hall), Don was legally allowed to stay with us. He may have seemed rebellious and dangerous to the outside world, but he was genuinely warm and gentle with the people he knew and trusted, and above all with the animals he cared for.

Laura, my girlfriend at the time, was a promising trainer. Joy was our general manager and the backbone of the company. After the accounting was done, and all the calls returned, she was out the door helping the others to prepare the food for the nursery animals. Ruth ran the house, and Ma Pud cooked for us.

The youngest member of our team was Maria, a tiny pixie of a girl. She had come to us one day from up north, alone, introverted, distrustful, and depressed. She was carrying a knapsack bigger than she was, and looking for a new way of life. From the day she arrived, I knew that this sensitive and dedicated young woman could benefit deeply from the love and tranquillity the animals had to offer. And she did. As time went on, we learned that Maria had a beautiful, lilting singing voice, and she brightened the kitchen and the forest with her gift.

Most people think of Southern California as sun and sand, a paradise for surfers and beach bunnies, but that's not always the case. In our second year, although it hadn't snowed for years, the area was hit by an unprecedented storm. Suddenly the temperature began to drop and then there was snow, enormous amounts of snow. Not just little white flakes that melted before they touched the ground; it was coming so thick and so fast that you could hardly see your hand in front of your face. It raged out of control almost immediately, and caught us totally unprepared.

By the sixth day, the situation was getting dire. We hadn't been in contact with the outside world for five days. The electric lines were down, the telephone was dead, and the twisting two-lane road leading down the mountain to Thousand Oaks, seventeen miles away, was impassable. Food for the animals, especially the meat eaters, would soon run out, and the human food supply was also running short.

Even the relentlessly optimistic Ted seemed a bit depressed as he came in from checking on the animals in the compound.

"We're just holding our own," he said. "Everybody's dry, at least for now—but I've got to tell you, Ralph, it's getting scary."

I put my hand on his shoulder. "I know, but hey—a group like us. . . ."

"I know," Ted said, momentarily cheered. "It's no problem!"

But actually, we did have a problem. The house was enormous and required a tremendous amount of firewood to keep it warm, and we were running low. We needed to bring in a large supply if we were going to make it through the storm.

"I found an enormous dead tree down the mountainside about

three hundred yards from the house," I said. "We could sure use it for firewood, but it's going to be tough work bringing it up to the house. Do you want to give it a try?"

"Yeah, sure," Ted said with the renewed enthusiasm that a sense of purpose will give you. As I put on my jacket I yelled, "Whoever wants to help haul a tree for firewood, let's go!"

I heard affirmative responses throughout the house. We zipped up our parkas and headed out into the blizzard. For three hours, Ted, Maria, Don, Joy, Laura, Ruth, and I pushed and pulled, fell and slid, trying to haul that tree up the mountain, but for all our efforts we gained only about a hundred feet. It was clear that our plan wasn't going to work without modifications.

Suddenly I got an idea. "Let's get the horses and a couple of ropes—that'll help."

Ted and I headed for the barn and chose two stallions to ride. Stud was built more like a racehorse, with sleek lines, long legs, and delicate features, while Son was a roping quarter and looked like a bulldozer, with his thick chest, short legs, and powerful muscles. Midnight and Mollie, the two girls, were left behind, warm and comfortable in the barn.

We tied ropes around the tree and threw a loop around the saddle horns, put our own shoulders to the task, and gave a click of the tongue to the horses to pull. And pull they did. They strained into their chest plates, with steam pouring from their nostrils. Sometimes they slipped, and at times even fell. But, together with the team, they managed to get the oak up to the back door of the house.

Now we just needed to get it inside. I didn't see any reason to fix something that was working, so I rode Son through the door and into the main room and threw a new loop over the roots of the tree. With all of us pushing, we managed to get the roots right up to the edge of the fireplace. Dismounting, I grabbed the roots; everybody followed suit, and we raised that section enough to thrust the whole base of the tree into the huge fireplace. While the main room was nearly thirty feet wide from the fireplace to the door, that tree was thirty-eight feet long! As a result, a good portion of it stuck out the back door. Nobody minded. We were content with the fact that at least we could have a fire, and we knew that the roots would eventually burn down. We planned to gradually inch the tree into the fireplace until we could close the back door.

After I had put Son in his stall, I walked over to the compound. Zamba was pacing anxiously in his cage, anticipating another night of howling winds and freezing rain. When he saw me, he jumped up against the chain links, all nine feet and 528 pounds of him, and looked down at me, begging for a little comfort and love. I couldn't resist, so I opened the door and went in. He exploded with joy, running all over his cage.

At my command, he rolled to a stop and lay upside down at my feet, looking up at me with his huge golden eyes. When I reached down to put on his leash, he pulled me down on top of him with his paws and proceeded to give me a rather raspy lick across my face. God, what a great lion—what a great friend!

As long as he had me to play with, Zamba loved the snow, and took great delight in jumping into a drift and scattering the soft, powdery flakes. He was soon covered with a heavy coat of it, and he seemed to like his new white cape, showing it off by high-stepping majestically.

We arrived at the house covered from head to toe. A blazing fire was going, and everybody was huddled around it. Everybody had brought a blanket and pillow, and had secured his or her own territory near the tree that was sticking out of the fireplace. I put a bowl of milk down for Zamba to enjoy and joined the rest of the crew. Maria, Laura, and Joy had brought some baby animals up from the compound to ensure their safety from the cold, and we turned some of them loose on the tree.

Jacks and Kabor, both tiny and delicate, lived together in the nursery. Jacks was a squirrel monkey, with beautiful dark eyes, elflike ears, and a long tail that he curled up between his legs and over his shoulder when he wasn't using it for balance. He would often fall asleep holding it like a pillow. Kabor, a marmoset, was a bit smaller, with a white tuft of hair sprouting from the top of his head. He could always be found nestled close to Jacks.

Stinky and Bandit were also roommates and clearly cared for each other very much, although their personalities were quite different. Stinky, as you might have guessed, was a skunk. She liked to sleep a lot, and her raccoon buddy Bandit was always waking her up by jumping right onto the middle of her back, and Stinky would arch her tail at him, but thankfully, her scent glands had already been removed.

The four little animals scampered up and down the tree, enjoying its many hide-and-seek opportunities. They weren't the only ones. Among the branches and along the bark, ants had set out on a long journey to gather what food information they could, sending it back to the colony through the ranks at incredible speed. Some ladybugs were setting up house in a niche of dried leaves and twigs. Hordes of beetles clambered everywhere, decorated with red, blue, and green dots and stripes, gorgeous patterns of color. All of them were moving away from the advancing flames, and the slow-burning wood gave most of them the chance to make it to safety.

Unfortunately, that meant into the house. We had to step lightly for the next few days, as the multicolored beetles, columns of ants, and even an old daddy longlegs were all scampering for new quarters.

The blaze of the fire cast a cavelike glow in the room; all else was pitch-black. I looked around at my family, and saw that they, too, recognized the special quality of this moment. The Bible says that a tree is a symbol of wisdom. So it may be, but it also gives of itself—its strength, its security, and its protection. I really understood that as we gathered around the tree in our great room that night. To touch it was to tune in to the soul of nature, to become one with the infinite.

Joy snuggled down in her comforter. "I feel guilty," she said quietly. "With all the stress and worry, I still feel wonderful, and I don't understand it."

Zamba laid his great head in my lap.

"You feel as the animals do, Joy. You're part of a group, not an individual now," I said. "You know the difference between man and the animals? If a person on a crowded street in New York sees a runaway car coming in his direction, he panics and runs, knocking into others who remain unaware of the impending danger. But if groups of antelope are feeding on the veldt and one sees a lion approaching, the whole group reacts. They run in the same direction without knocking into one another, because they are listening to a universal 'mind.'

"Animals do this naturally, in emergency and in tranquillity. I think we're so close to our animals right now, and our love for them is so strong that we've crossed over, to their dominion. Wouldn't it be amazing if everyone in the world could feel like this, just once in their lives?"

It was a long speech for me, and it was followed by a long, heavy silence. Everyone was deep in thought, sharing in the moment. Then, from a pile of blankets, bodies, and animals came someone's voice:

"No problem."

Everyone broke up.

Finally we fell asleep. When a chill woke us, we would push the tree a little farther into the fireplace, where it would blaze anew. We repeated this ritual until we could finally close the back door.

In the middle of the night I woke up and walked quietly over to the window. I looked out at a frozen white world. A bright moon lit the cloudless sky and the countryside below with an eerie glow. Nothing moved, and there was nothing to give away the existence of life out there. I was moved, watching nature sleep. After a few minutes, I turned toward the fire, and our mother protector, the tree. Territories had been forgotten, as the sleeping animals cuddled against the warmth of the tree. The hot bright coals threw light against the tree branches and reflected them against the ceiling.

I felt the chill. Zamba was curled up, kittenlike, and I was happy to hurry back to his warmth, snuggling up under his mane.

15

Our sense of peace was not to last. By dawn the storm had started to rage again. Food supplies were getting critically low. We were feeding five hundred pounds of meat a day just to the big cats—the lions, tigers, and leopards—and tons of alfalfa and oat hay went to the hoofed stock.

I was deep in thought, lost in calculations for rationing the food among the animals, when I heard someone scream. Nobody likes to hear a scream at the best of times, but a scream on a wild animal ranch is absolutely bloodcurdling, and my mind went to the worst possible scenario. Was something—or somebody—being killed? Hearing that scream set my adrenaline racing, and I got to the window as fast as I could.

In the snow-covered valley by the horse barn, I saw a small human figure running, screaming, and falling in the heavy snow. I raced out the door and slipped and slid myself the quarter-mile distance to the barn. It was Maria. When I got to her, she was hysterical. She threw her arms around me, crying and shaking. I wiped the snow from her face and tried to calm her down as best I could. I half carried her back to the horse barn, from where, according to her tracks, she had just come.

The smell of horses and hay filled my nostrils as soon as we entered the barn—and then I saw them. Our horses were lying all around us. Some of the seven were already dead, and some were clearly dying. To this day, the image is burned on my brain. I stood there, stunned, as my mind raced over the possibilities.

Then I ran to Stud, to Mollie, to Midnight. I had known these horses for a long time and they, like all the other animals, had become a part of our family. Maria had gone over to Midnight, her favorite. She had spent hours grooming and riding her. She was lying flat, every breath a labor. Together Maria and I tried to get Midnight to stand, but despite everything we were doing to help her, she just couldn't make it to her feet.

The barn door burst open again and Joy, Ted, Laura, and Don were there with us. Their faces all registered the sudden shock I had felt just moments before. Each went to his or her favorite horse and pleaded with it to get up. Three or four of us would all pitch in as one. Pulling, hauling, bracing with our backs, we would finally get one animal to stand for a moment, only to have it topple over again. We fetched blankets and lanterns and built a small fire. I racked my brain to figure out what had happened. The only thing I could think of was food poisoning.

I walked over to the hay, and saw it: mold. The rain and snow must have caught the edge of the hay. But the horror behind me was still a mystery. I had seen horses eat moldy hay before, and they hadn't died from it! Whatever it was, we needed to know what to do. I decided to send Ted on a mission to find out whether the hay was truly bad, and also to bring back dearly needed supplies. I would stay at the ranch, and try to keep everyone calm. I called the group together. Except for Maria, who wouldn't leave Midnight, we huddled near the fire.

"Look, Ted, it's up to you, buddy. The snow here has stopped, at least for now. It may be the only chance we've got to get you down."

"I don't mind going," he said, "but I don't think old Betsy can make it up the driveway to the main road. The tires will just spin out." Betsy was our beloved truck.

Don, who rarely spoke, suggested that we modify the car chains to fit with the truck chains for added traction. Laura suggested we use Son.

"He didn't eat whatever made the others sick; he's fine. Use him to help to pull the truck out to the main road. It's all downhill from there."

"Okay," I said, "but Ted, if we get you up and over the driveway, you're on your own for seventeen miles downhill on a road you probably won't even be able to see."

"It's no problem," Ted said, his face somber and determined.

A light snow had started to fall as Ted climbed into the truck. He turned her engine over; she sputtered, then jumped and roared into action. I jumped on Son's back while Don tied a rope to the truck's bumper. I tied the other end to the saddle horn. Meanwhile the rest of our crew had lined the road ahead with brush and twigs. The double chains looked awkward, but strong. I gave the signal; the motor roared, Son pulled, everybody pushed, and off old Betsy went, backfiring, slipping and sliding, chains biting into the wet mush.

Before we knew it, Ted was over the rise and onto what we believed was the road. I unhitched the rope from the bumper. With a wave and a honk, Ted was off, the truck spinning sideways, weaving and sliding, down the mountain. We watched until he disappeared.

The plan was insane. How was he ever going to make it down the hill in one piece—let alone back up? But we had no other options.

The storm started picking up as we walked back to the house. It was as though the powers above had held the storm back to give Ted a chance. I tried not to think of the consequences if he didn't make it.

We set to work making the remaining horses as comfortable as possible. Mollie was dead, and Stud was going fast. We separated the bad hay from the good, throwing out every strand we thought could possibly have been contaminated. When that sad work was done, I left Maria and Don to tend to the horses' needs, and the rest of us went out to feed, bed down, and water the other animals.

The meat had run out, so to feed the big cats we had to kill laying chickens from the roost. Feeding a two- or three-pound chicken to a lion is like feeding an apple to an elephant, but at least their stomachs wouldn't be totally empty.

When the sun set that evening on the cold, isolated valley, Maria refused to come up to the house, insisting on staying with Midnight. I left her enough wood to keep a fire going all night. We went to bed early, knowing that we'd need our energy, but no one slept very well.

Dawn broke cold and gray. I threw on an old army jacket and headed outside. The crunch of the snow under my feet was the only sound I heard on the walk to the barn. The night's snowfall had caused drifts to pile up around the barn door, but since the snow was fresh and soft it yielded to my push. I stepped quietly in, prepared for the worst.

The fire in the barn had gone out, and everything was still. My eyes moved from one silent form to another. Was that a sign of life? A tremble? Some of the horses lay in the shadows, others had beams from the morning sun stretched across their faces. Odd that we die with our eyes open—cold, glazed eyes stared at me from everywhere. I looked for Midnight. She was lying near the burned-out fire. Maria was sleeping nestled in Midnight's forelegs. Her arm was cocked up over the animal's neck; one hand was hidden in the mane as though she had gone to sleep stroking it. I touched Midnight, and found her body was cold and hard. My God, she was dead! I had no way of knowing if she'd died before Maria had fallen asleep or after, and my heart broke at the thought that this was what she would wake up to.

To be in love with nature and so attached to her animals—it hurts more than anything when they go! I knelt down and brushed the hair from Maria's eyes. She stirred. I shook her gently, and she slowly woke up, her eyes shimmering with tears. She knew: Midnight had died during the night in her arms. I held her as she wept softly, her body cold and shaking.

There was not a single movement anywhere else in the barn. They were all dead.

I hardly remember anything about that day; thankfully, there was a lot of relentlessly hard work to do to keep the other animals comfortable. And three days after we'd watched Ted disappear over the mountain, we heard a car horn. We rushed outside just in time to see Ted coming over the ridge, honking and skidding all the way. He had made it! The truck was piled high with equipment, food supplies, and medicine.

He also brought news about our hay. The vet had analyzed the mold and found it to be botulism, one of the most deadly of all poisons. Nothing could have helped the horses. We always stored different shipments of hay separately to ensure freshness, so we could very easily isolate the bad batch and feed the rest to the other livestock.

Ted had brought as much meat as the truck would carry,

enough to hold us for a few days. That night, everybody feasted. After dinner, Ted took me aside.

"I almost didn't make it," he said. "I came close to going over many times. Look, Ralph, Dr. Freeman realizes the problem we're having, and he thought—" He stopped. "I heard on the news that there's no sign of the storm letting up." He put his head down.

"What are you trying to tell me, Ted?" I asked. "Just say it."

Ted adjusted his Western hat, pulling it low over his forehead. "The cats aren't going to make it, Ralph, unless—"

"Unless what?!"

"Unless we feed the horse meat to them."

My mouth hung open in horror. "My God, man, what are you saying? Feed them Mollie and Stud and Midnight? You're crazy! We'll find another way," I said, and walked off.

Ted yelled after me, "Doc said the meat won't hurt them—just don't feed them the insides!"

Ted knew—as I eventually came to realize—that there was no other way. The next few days were murderously cold and wet, and the situation on the ranch became desperate. Courageous Ted approached me once more about the horse meat, and deep down I knew he was right. I called a meeting by the fire and told the group what the vet had suggested. In the flickering light I could see the shock on their faces, the lowered eyes. Yet everyone understood, particularly after Maria raised her head and said, "Midnight is long gone from that cold, dead body lying down there in the barn, and I'm sure she would agree that if it's to help her animal friends, then it's okay."

I had all of the knives sharpened, and Ted, Don, and I prepared to leave, but the women stopped us at the door. They, too, were dressed in boots, heavy jackets, wool scarves, and gloves, and they were going to help. Even tiny Maria could not be talked out of it.

I used the old truck to pull some of the carcasses out of the barn, and each person went to work. Maria would let no one help her. The job was tremendous for a big man, let alone for a very small woman. By evening, snow had started to fall again. Everyone else had finished, and only Maria and I were left in the barn. I pretended to be doing some work around the barn, because I didn't want her to be alone.

Maria looked up at me, her tears like small white snowflakes on her cheeks.

"Ralph," she said, in a voice barely audible against the wind, "could I . . . ?" She wiped her eyes against the sleeve of her coat. I could tell that what she had to say was difficult for her.

"I mean, if the weather is okay, could I ride Son tomorrow?"

I couldn't hide my tears, but they were tears of joy. I knew then that Maria was really going to make it through this horrendous ordeal.

"Sure, honey," I said, "if the weather is okay."

There was the slightest movement of her lip and chin, and she went back to her chore.

The snowflakes had become larger and were falling thicker and faster, but a slight wisp of warm breeze caught me off guard. It was the kind of dry wind that comes in from the desert and sweeps down across the valley, and when I felt it, I knew that the worst weather was behind us.

I went back up the hill to the house to get Zamba for a little exercise, and although I had every intention of getting as far away from the barn as possible, he kept wanting to head in that direction, and I figured Maria could probably use the company.

As we approached, I could hear her singing. Zamba's whole bearing changed, and he tasted the air, clearly confused by the messages he was getting.

I will never, ever forget what I saw when I came over that rise. She was sitting inside Midnight's abdominal cavity, wearing a massive pea coat with the sleeves rolled up and her collar pulled up around her neck, quietly cutting as the light from a small candle flickered against the horse's rib walls. The blood mingled with the snow. She was sobbing as she sang.

Zamba, in all his wisdom, headed over in her direction. I tried to keep him away, but the emotional weight of the day meant that I didn't have much struggle left in me, and I knew Maria could handle herself. There was no need. Zamba lay down beside her in the bloodstained snow, and as she cut and sang and cried, she would periodically cut a piece of the meat for him and feed it to him from her hands.

It was one of the heaviest things I have ever seen in my life, and at least part of me recoiled from the dreadfulness of it: Midnight and Zamba had been friends. But I also realized that Maria was responding to a higher call. Through her generosity, she was really closer than any of us to achieving true communion with the animals and with nature. I learned a great deal from her on that sad day.

16

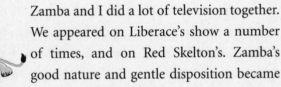 Zamba and I did a lot of television together. We appeared on Liberace's show a number of times, and on Red Skelton's. Zamba's good nature and gentle disposition became well-known, and we received calls from charitable organizations asking if he would come and help raise funds for a variety of worthwhile causes. Many of them involved children, and we were happy to help schools for orphans, the children's wards at various hospitals, the March of Dimes, the Red Cross, and many more. Zamba sported ribbons around his neck, wore paper hats, and even accepted a beautiful hand-stitched saddlelike jacket from an organization of the elderly. He visited homes for the sick, old, and infirm, attended Christmas parties, and once even had his mane whitened with baby powder so he could wear a Santa Claus hat.

Sometimes, in the beginning, I was anxious about exploiting him that way. When I saw him in a paper hat, I thought, *How can the king of the jungle wear such foolish things?* But Zamba's generosity taught me that a true monarch is humble, and not above doing things for the less fortunate or giving to the needy. The appreciative look in the eyes of a sick child made our experiences helping them meaningful.

I often worked on a television show with Betty White, a dear friend and one of the world's finest comediennes. Whenever she needed an animal on the show, she would call me and I would bring over whichever animal fit the circumstances.

Zamba was one of the audience's favorites, and he appeared a number of times. One day I received the following letter from an admirer:

Dear Sir,

My name is Dawn. I am sixteen, and I have been blind all my life. It's okay. I mean, if I haven't ever seen before then I don't know what I'm missing, right? I feel sorry for those people who once saw and then had their eyesight taken away. How horrible!

I think I know what many people look like. I can recognize most by their voices and their faces. They all have noses and mouths and eyes. Anyhow, the one thing that has always intrigued me is nature. When I hear people talk about it, it seems so big. I mean the sky and clouds flowing up there and then there are valleys, mountains, and the animals. How does one see a cloud? The only things I see are those I can touch. How can you touch a mountain or a cloud? Someday I hope to see a clown. But they mimic and I can't see them mimic. I read a lot. Of course, only in Braille. I do pretty well with it.

Last year I read a story about a lion. This lion ruled the jungle and all the animals in it. He was huge, with a large mane, long fangs, and an extremely loud roar.

I saw you, well, heard you, on Betty White's show with

your lion Zamba. Lions are my favorite of all the animals, especially after I read this story. In the book he was very wise. He protected the innocent, and fought for the rights of others.

The real reason for this letter is to ask if I could see Zamba. (To see him I would have to touch him.) I have tried to figure out how he looks but I just can't.

I would be most grateful if you would allow me to meet, and hopefully, touch Zamba. It would allow me to see him.

Sincerely,
Dawn

I was taken aback by this letter, and by this young woman's sweetness, innocence, and love for nature. I wrote immediately to tell her that Zamba and I would be honored to have her come and visit.

And so she did. She arrived on a beautiful Sunday afternoon when the sky was clear and blue, and nature was in its full glory. A black Cadillac came to a halt at the end of our driveway, and out stepped a beautiful girl with such confidence and self-assurance that I could hardly believe she was indeed blind. About five-six, and slender, she had a thick head of long blond hair that hung down to the small of her back. I was surprised to see that she wore no glasses; most sightless people do. It would have been a shame; her deep gray eyes were clear and bright, and her gaze was steady and calm. A man stood next to her.

"Hello, there," I offered as I approached the car. Dawn turned toward the sound of my voice, and her smile was absolutely radiant. She was facing into the sun, and completely illuminated by it, but she did not have to shade her eyes, as others would have. "I'm Ralph, Zamba's friend."

"Hi. I'm Dawn and this is my father, Daniel."

I had expected him to handle the greeting.

We sat outside on the patio and spoke of many things. Her father was a quiet man, learned and polite. He felt they were intruding, and it took me great effort to persuade him otherwise.

"I'm so excited! What do I do when I meet your friend?" she said, referring to Zamba.

"What do you normally do when you meet someone?" I asked.

"Do I shake his paw?" she said.

I laughed along with her. "No," I said. "Just stay calm and let him come to you. He'll smell you, and then rub up against you. Try to brace your legs so he doesn't accidentally knock you down, but don't worry; we'll be there to support you."

I noticed that, instead of a cane, she carried a hiking stick. It was perhaps five feet long, thicker at the top than at the bottom, and was covered with many inscriptions and carved figures.

"Where did you get such a beautiful walking stick?" I asked, as we walked over to Zamba's enclosure.

"From a Scottish friend," she said. "I asked him what a mountain looked like. He tried to describe it, but got a bit frustrated: 'If you can't see a mountain then you can bloody well climb one.' So he took me to Mount Wilson and we climbed it! The view, I felt, was breathtaking."

This was a remarkable girl, I thought.

"Well, best not to have it around," I said, laying the stick on the sofa. I didn't want anything to go wrong.

She nodded. "Yes, yes. Of course. I have never been so excited in all my life," she said. I could hear her breath, coming short and fast. I smiled at her father, who looked more than a little nervous.

I excused myself and went to get Zam. He greeted me with his usual "urrph!" I put the chain around his neck, careful to make sure that it lay under his mane. Sometimes, if he was in a playful mood, he could intentionally slip out of it, and I didn't want anything to go wrong. I wanted this experience to be as wonderful as Dawn imagined it could be. I had bathed Zamba just a few hours earlier; for her to see him, she would have to feel his body, and I wanted his fur to be as soft as down.

Zamba had a unique way of looking at people. Some animals will look at the person as a whole entity, taking in his whole body. Zamba always looked at a person's face, and waited, as though he were reading the person's thoughts. It was a very intense experience. When one person looks long and hard at another person, there can be a tendency to become nervous and turn away. Zamba caused many of the people he met to do just that. Some people would look over their shoulder, thinking he was looking at something behind them. He made many people uneasy; they knew he was studying them, and most wondered what he was thinking.

I realized that he liked *knowing* people, not just meeting them, and he could tell a lot about them by their touch, their smell, and their body language. And although he was polite to everyone, there were definitely some people that he didn't care for at all. With them, he would flick his tail, turn around, and look the other way. He allowed them to touch him only because I asked it of him.

There were others whom he accepted right away. If he did his "augh," then rubbed against their leg and allowed them to touch him, they were in!

We walked up to Dawn and her father. Zamba stood directly in front of Dawn. Strangely, he didn't look at her face, but focused on an area above her head. He seemed to be watching something that I couldn't see.

"He's here, isn't he? I know it. I can feel him," Dawn said, with a tremor in her voice. Before I could answer, she continued. "He's so big." She was sweating. I looked at her father. We both realized she hadn't touched him yet! Zamba and I approached within a few inches of her.

Then he lowered his head.

"You can kneel down, Dawn," I said. "He's directly in front of you."

Normally I would have a person approach from the side, but Zamba seemed not quite his usual self. I was a little confused, and stood close in case he pushed into her. She slowly lowered herself, hands outstretched, feeling for the ground until she was on her knees. Her face was at the same level as his.

"Okay, now reach up and let him smell your hand."

She slowly raised her hand. Zamba sniffed, then raised his head and grimaced. Lions do this to get the full impact of an odor, the same way a wine connoisseur will allow air into his mouth with the wine, to fully savor the bouquet.

"Now you can touch him," I said.

"Where?"

"Wherever you like."

As soon as her hand touched his mane, she whimpered, and exhaled with a small, quiet cry. It was as though she wasn't breathing until the moment she touched him.

Zamba stood still, looking into her face—perhaps her eyes. She buried her hand in his thick fur, and she closed her eyes as her fingers traveled, seeing all that she had dreamed of, all that her mind needed her to see. She never stopped whimpering. Leaning forward, she laid her head against his mane.

Zamba had never been one to stand when he could lie down. Lions are like that—lazy. But this time he stood, quiet.

Dawn raised herself up and began to trace her hands down his back until she reached his tail. Touch a lion at the base of his tail, and he will flick in irritation, like a scorpion. Not today. His tail lay quiet, without a twitch. When she got back to his face, he slowly lay down, and put his head in her lap. Dawn closed her eyes as one does when praying, or kissing a loved one.

She had no fear; she had completely entered into his world. Her fingers traced the area around his huge round eyes, felt his ears buried down in his thick mane, and stroked the long, straight bridge of his nose. She pushed her fingers under his upper lip and ran her fingers up and down his huge fangs. Her small, delicate hands floated over his entire body.

"You are so big!" she whispered. "Much bigger than I had thought. You are the Lion God in my book."

She laid her head on his mane and hugged him.

"It's time to go now, Dawn," her father said.

As if awakening from a dream, she kissed Zamba's nose, and he licked her hand. They both got to their feet.

"Good-bye, my hero," she said, and gave him a huge hug. He returned with a gentle nuzzle.

Zamba and I watched as the two of them walked to the car.

Looking back over her shoulder she said, "Thanks for letting me see you."

"Augh!" he answered.

Other events came our way that allowed us to demonstrate just how successful affection training could be. One day I received a call from a company with a Roman theme.

"Do you have any lions?"

"Ah! Well, yes, sure. What do you have in mind?" I asked.

"We want to build a very large float to represent the days of the Roman Olympics. You know, the Colosseum, Circus Maximus, and gladiators. We want to put the lions on the float with no cages, but we're concerned as to whether it will be safe. We called all the animal companies, including Jungleland, but everybody turned us down; they say it's too dangerous. Maybe we're asking too much. There will be about a million people lined along the route, and it's not entirely under our control. There will be children, balloons popping, bands—lots of noise and activity."

"A million people?" I blurted.

"Oh, sorry—I thought I'd told you. It's for the Rose Parade."

"*The Rose Parade?*" I paused.

"No problem," I said. "We can do it."

"Well, I'll take this to the committee, and if they approve, I'll get right back to you. Cheers."

I hoped I hadn't bitten off more then I could chew. It was a tall order and a big responsibility. If approved, this would be the first time in history that such a float would be allowed in the Rose Parade, and the lions would be just a few feet from the crowds. But I knew my animals and trainers, and I knew we could do it.

A couple of weeks later, the committee wrote me a very nice letter stating that they had reviewed the situation, had researched my company, and felt that we would be the best—the only—company they would allow to do it. The parade was about four months away. When we signed our contract, they showed us the multimillion-dollar insurance premium they had to pay to appease the Rose Bowl people.

They shipped us gladiator costumes for the trainers to wear. We had asked for them early so the trainers could get the lions used to the way that we looked in them. It was always odd to look out the window from my office to see gladiators, complete with feathered helmets, walking the lions through the property.

In preparation, we erected special caging to put in the back of pickup trucks, and used them to drive the lions through the busiest sections of town. We staged our own "parade" at the ranch with drums and our horses. Marching band music was played over loudspeakers, and we used garbage can lids as cymbals, banging them in cadence with the music. We drove the lions to every event being held in Los Angeles to get them accustomed to all the activity and excitement. We wanted to make sure none of the noises or smells would make them panic.

We figured we had achieved our goal when the lions slept through the commotion.

The day of the parade arrived. We were ready at four in the morning. Zamba and one of the other lions, Zamba Jr. (not directly related to Zamba, but of the same temperamental mold), were to ride up front on the float. Two of our other lions, Tammy and Leo, would ride behind. All the lions had been bathed and combed, and everything was set to go.

As we approached the downtown area, a motorcycle police escort helped us through the crowds. The float was as they had said—enormous. It was built to symbolize the Roman era of the Circus Maximus, with all its pomp. Roman columns rose high in the air. Marble steps led up to a mock remnant of the ancient Forum and gave one the feeling of being there. Thousands of flowers—red and white roses, marigolds, and carnations of all colors—covered the columns and the float itself.

We put the lions in their designated places. Each one was featured on a simulated marble rise so the huge crowds could see them, leashes hidden under their manes or decorated with flowers. As the parade started, each "gladiator" took position alongside the lions. Some of us walked along with the float, others stood on it, near the animals. We were all in full armor and carried a shield, whip, mace, or some sort of artificial weapon to set the mood. I positioned myself as close as I could to Zamba so he could see me at all times. Leading the float was a herald, the kind you'd have heard before the games started in the Roman Colosseum.

We were a huge hit. The hordes of people watching the parade went wild, screaming and applauding. Some did the famous thumbs up or down.

And I must say, we looked great. The lions were outstanding; they were thoroughly enjoying the ride, and you could tell. They stood or sat, looking down at their people like the kings they are. We didn't have a single problem.

The float won the award for its category, and the company sponsoring the float was ecstatic.

Afterward, back at the ranch, we all celebrated. The women, dressed in togas, had prepared a surprise Roman party for us. They had spread blankets, lit torches, and cooked up a true Roman feast, complete with the same marching band music that had been played in the parade. A special platform complete with torches at each corner was raised so the lions could sit and watch. We threw scraps of meat to them just as the Romans had done centuries ago. Some of the "gladiators" gave a go at a simulated fight. We ate with our hands, drank wine, and danced until the sun came up.

It was a one-of-a-kind performance. As far as I'm concerned, no one else has ever been able to match it.

17

Brini and Jack's phone call had changed my life completely. In the spring of 1960, my life was changed by another phone call.

"So sorry to ring you up on a Sunday morning, but we've only just found out about you, and it's most important that we speak." The voice at the other end of the line was quite formal.

"What can I do for you?" I asked, still working on my breakfast.

"I represent the Twentieth Century–Fox studio. I understand that you have lions?"

"Yes, we have quite few. What exactly do you need?"

"We have a film that requires a lion to work with a child. Can you do that?"

"Yes," I said.

"Yes? Yes? You're sure?" His voice had lost all its formality. "Can your lion actually *be* with a child and not, uh—not hurt her? I mean, really?" You would have thought I'd just delivered the Hope diamond.

"I have a lion that loves children."

"Is he big?"

"Yes, quite."

"Well then, can you bring him to the studios on Monday so you and your lion can meet the producer?"

"I can do that, but before you go, will you tell me exactly what they have in mind?"

The more I knew, the better prepared I'd be.

"All I know is that Sam Engel, the producer of the film *The Lion,* has put out a call around the world for a full-grown lion to star in the film. The animal has to be able to work safely with a child actress, and so far, no lion has been found that can fill the bill. Everybody they contacted said it was impossible, and that a lion would kill a child. The studio was in the process of constructing a mechanical lion when the actor Bill Holden recommended I call you. That's all I know. That, and they're going to be filming in Africa."

My heart started racing, and I struggled to keep my breath under control. We all have goals in life; things we want to do, places we want to see. My own most personal and passionately held goal was to go to Africa. I had wanted—I might even say needed—to go there since childhood. Something about that continent called me. I wasn't sure if it was the animals, the land, the people, or some combination of all three, but the desire was so strong in me that it kept me up at night.

The only thing I loved more than the idea of Africa were my lions, and the opportunity to see those two passions intersect was so incredible, it boggled my mind.

"Okay," I said, trying to sound professional. "Thanks for the information."

I confirmed the time and spent the rest of the day ecstatic about the possibility of getting the job. It also gave me great satisfaction to imagine getting a job that my main competitor, Jungleland, couldn't do.

Monday morning found me loading a scrubbed and immaculately brushed Zamba into my station wagon. I'll tell you—when you travel with a lion, doors open to you! When I pulled up to the studio gate, the guard took one look at Zamba and didn't even ask for my name, he just let us in. I unloaded Zam in the parking lot, clipped a leash on him, and headed for our destination, where a very nervous secretary pointed the way to the producer's office.

I pushed the button for the elevator. When the doors opened, the people on the elevator took one look at Zamba and fell over themselves trying to move as far back into the car as they could. I had to back Zamba halfway across the lobby before they would leave the elevator, and we had to race through the doors before they closed.

On our floor, a security guard stayed at a distance, but pointed out the door to the producer's office. He was kind enough to open it for us—although he held the handle with his fingertips and moved away fast.

We entered a huge office done in dark mahogany furniture against a thick, dark brown rug. At the end of the room was a large, fancy glass desk framed in ebony wood. It was a dark and depressing office, except for a large glass window with a view over the studio lot.

The glare coming in from the outside made seeing the man behind the desk almost impossible. The only thing you could see was the silhouette of another man smoking a cigar in front of the window. I had read that many executives put their desks in front of a window, so they see their visitors' faces without being seen themselves. They believe it gives them an advantage.

"Well, well, so this is the famous lion that will work with children," said the shadow at the desk.

"Yes, sir, this is Zamba."

There was no handshake. I figured he was afraid of the lion coming too close to him.

"He won't pee on my carpet, will he, young man?"

"No, sir."

"What makes you so sure he won't eat the kid?"

"He's experienced with children, sir."

He was quiet for some time. Then, "Okay, tomorrow you'll meet the kid and see if she and the lion get along. If he can do the job, fine. If not, we don't need either one of you."

Then he waved his hand at me, as if he were dismissing a servant. I left the office feeling put down. This person knew nothing about us, and he'd treated us as if we were less than he was. I found out later that the man I was talking to was not the producer, but a production head with a lot of power, and no one spoke well of him. I was too young myself to recognize his strategy: what he was really saying was "We don't need you, so you'd better lower your price or there won't be a job at all." I knew they had no lion, but I also knew that they were threatening to use a mechanical one.

I received a call the next day that a meeting had been arranged, and I should take Zamba to meet Pamela Franklin, the little girl actress.

We met Pam and her mother on the back lot of the studio. Another production head was also there. He was very polite, and there were introductions all around.

Pam was a delight: a vibrant and bright little lady who captured Zamba's and my heart immediately. The two of them got along famously. Obviously, I was very careful to make sure that nothing happened that might scare Pam. Sometimes Zamba's natural exuberance could be a bit overwhelming, and I would have to remind him to cool it. I told Pam and her mother about how Zam had come to live with me, and showed Pam where to stand when she was around Zamba, how he liked to be brushed (in only one direction!), how to walk him on a leash—even how to hug him. I could see they would be just fine together. She learned quickly, and I knew that it would be a joy to work with her.

After I put Zamba in the station wagon, Pam's mother called me over.

"Mr. Helfer, you and Zamba are wonderful, and I am looking forward to the film. I want you to know, though, that every night I go to sleep, I will be praying that nothing goes wrong. I am a mother who loves her daughter very much and, well, I guess I'm sort of a worry bird. I just want you to know that I trust you with my daughter's life. Please be careful."

With this she kissed me on the cheek. I understood at that moment how much of a responsibility this was: the life of someone else's little girl, someone's daughter, was in my hands.

It sounds ridiculous, but up to then, it had never really occurred to me that Zamba would hurt anybody. I was still sure in my core that he wouldn't, but now I would be taking extra precautions. Her reminder rang in my ears for the duration of the job.

A few days later I returned to the office with my proposal. The studio had requested more lions. The production head was as obnoxious as he'd been the day we first met when I handed him the contract I had drawn up. I had spent considerable time on it, figuring in what it would cost to take the trainers, Zamba, and the two other lions that they'd requested for a six-month stay in Kenya. It was a considerable sum, but it was very fair.

He ripped opened the envelope and looked at the figures.

"What the hell is this?" he screamed, screwing the paper up into a ball and throwing it at me.

I stood there in complete shock. Was this guy actually talking to me like this? I'd never seen anything like his behavior in a professional setting.

"What is this shit?"

I tried to explain my reasons for the numbers in the contract.

"Out! Out! Get the fuck out!"

I left, totally distraught, my dreams of Africa falling away before my eyes. How could this happen? Pam and Zamba were great together, and the contract I'd offered them was more than fair.

Next morning I received a call from the other man I'd met. He asked me to come back and bring a fresh contract. I did. He didn't make any excuses for the production head's actions—he just took my contract and signed right there! Apparently he was second in command and had the authority to sign.

"See you on the set." He smiled.

I was to find out that this was that particular production head's way—and the way of a lot of the hardballing executives around Hollywood. If they could pressure you into taking a deal for less than you were worth, they would. But they didn't have much room with me. There was only one Zamba, and they knew it.

18

The next week passed in a blur. I couldn't believe that Zamba and I were going to Africa together. But I should learn not to count my chickens before they hatch; we almost didn't make it there.

The Sunday after I signed the papers, I woke up slowly, aware of a heavy weight pressing me into the mattress. It felt as though a car had slipped off its jack, pinning me to the ground. I didn't panic. Zamba never could sleep on his side of the bed.

I managed to slip myself out from under his massive frame, making a mental note to give him a bath later—he needed it. After a quick shower, I dressed. Zamba, now lying diagonally across the bed, was still asleep. The snoring was serious.

I kicked the bed. "Zam! Come on! Up and out!"

He opened one eye, his huge mane matted to the back of his head. He looked as though he'd been out for a wild night on the town. I headed for the kitchen, enjoying a brief moment of appreciation for my life. *Isn't this great?* I thought. True, I didn't have a lot of money—in fact, very little. But I had the animals, and a unique way of life.

I heard a thud from upstairs—Zamba getting out of bed. He dragged himself sleepily into the kitchen, ignoring the yapping of the dog. He tripped over Speedy the tortoise, banged the back door screen open with his head, and headed for his favorite tree, which was starting to show the use.

I had recently fastened a steel cable about eight feet off the ground between two oak trees. The ground there had been raked and cleaned, and covered with fresh heavy cedar chips. I fastened Zamba's chain to a clip and then attached the clip to a ring that slid the length of the cable. This allowed Zamba to exercise the full length of the cable. If he decided to rest, the cedar chips would absorb any dampness, as well as keep him clean. Once on the cable, he shook himself again. Then, feeling as cocky as a puppy, he proceeded to race up and down the run, grunting and cavorting and just plain feeling good. I left him to warm himself and relax in the sun.

I wasn't alone. A few months before, a beautiful blond former model named Toni had shown up on my doorstep with two bear cubs tearing up the inside of her car. A ranger had killed their mother after she had menaced some tourists, and Toni, a real animal lover, had saved the cubs. But they were proving a little more than she could handle, and she wanted to know if I could help. I could, and did—and the sparks had flown between the two of us. She was fascinated by my life on the ranch, and insisted that I teach her everything I could. She was incredibly nurturing and warm, and the animals—especially Zamba—had taken to her immediately. It was as if she had been there forever.

Heading back to the compound, Toni and I went to work on a minor repair in Raunchy the jaguar's cage. It took only a few minutes to complete, and I put the last clamp on the chain-link fence as Toni headed for the kitchen to prepare breakfast, and returned Raunchy to his cage. Then I headed for the house. By the aroma, I could tell that Toni had the bacon and eggs well on the way. I went up to wash off as much of the sweat and dirt as I could, but as I turned off the faucet, I was suddenly hit by a wave of terror. Something was wrong.

Zamba!

I raced toward the kitchen.

"Zamba!" I screamed. Toni joined me and we ran toward the front door, crashing it open. "Oh, my God!"

The worst sight imaginable greeted our eyes.

"Dear God! Zamba!"

He was hanging by his neck over the steel cable, bent and lifeless, his head on one side, his body draped on the other, his hind section and tail dragging on the ground. Somehow, he had run around the oak tree, leaped eight feet up and over the wire, and had gotten caught.

As we ran to him, my mind was racing. How long had he been there? A minute? Five? Maybe even ten! His gorgeous, lifeless eyes stared at me. I touched them. They were sticky and unblinking.

I grabbed the clip to release the pressure from around Zamba's neck, but the tension was too strong. Toni and I tried to lift him over the wire to release the pressure of the chain around his neck, but his weight was too much for us.

I was frantic. We had to do something, now! But what?

I ran around the other side and, reaching over, grabbed his mane, one leg, and the bulk of his body and pulled for all I was worth—an impossible task.

"Come on, big fella!" I gasped.

Toni got underneath, and we gave it all we had. The enormous body moved, slid, swayed. I felt numbing pain as something tore in my arm. I pulled. Toni pushed. The balance shifted. Zamba's lifeless body teetered and then fell on me, knocking me flat.

I scrambled out from underneath him and, digging my hand into his mane, found the chain that was tight around his throat, choking off his windpipe. I squeezed the clip to release the pressure, and the whole chain popped off.

We pried Zamba's mouth open. His tongue and gums were white. Then I tapped his eye . . . no response.

"He's dead, Toni. Zamba's dead." The emotion was too much for me, and I burst into tears. "My Zamba! My baby—he couldn't! He can't. Please, dear God!!" He had been my mentor, my guide into the world of nature, my companion.

"We shouldn't have left him!" Toni sobbed.

We, like everybody else, had always tied our animals out at the ranch. There had never been a problem. This was some kind of freak accident.

Toni wrapped her arms around Zamba and hugged him as if her heart would break. Her weight pressed air from his lungs. When I heard it, I flung my full weight on his body, and again another small volume of air burst forth.

"Toni, honey, press together with me."

He was so huge that it took the full pressure of both our bodies to force the release of air from his lungs.

"Oh, Ralph, can it really help?"

"I don't know—but we have to try something!"

We were exhausted, but we wouldn't give up. For twenty minutes we pushed and released. I kept Zamba's mouth open, his tongue out, to free the passageway, but the only result of all our pushing was total exhaustion on our part. We lay there, Toni with her head in Zamba's mane, whimpering softly. I had my head buried in his chest, too grief-stricken to move.

"It's no use," I said.

Then I heard it! I pressed my ear tightly to his chest and listened.

"What's wrong, Ralph?"

"Sshh!" I whispered.

Then I heard it again! A far-off, slow, nearly inaudible beat. A heartbeat!

"Oh my God, it's beating!"

I heard it down there, in that mess of hair. Inside that great body, I heard it. I started to rub Zamba all over to help his circulation. Toni joined in. Our fatigue fell away as we grabbed all four of his feet, rolled him over onto his other side, and continued rubbing. A quick look in his mouth told me that his color was coming back.

I had Toni bring blankets from the house. I wrapped them all around his body for heat while she went to call the vet.

"He's on the way!" she yelled, running back. We hugged and kissed Zamba and each other. I slowly reached up toward Zamba's eye and, taking a deep breath, touched it. It blinked! Dear God! He was alive! Both Toni and I began to cry again, shedding tears of joy and of deep, heartfelt gratitude.

When the vet arrived, he immediately administered intravenous injections and stimulants and started glucose and a saline drip. Artificial heat was applied to keep Zamba's temperature up.

"What happened, Ralph?" the vet asked as he worked.

I told him what I thought had happened.

"How long were you away?"

"Just a matter of minutes!"

"Has this ever happened to you before?"

"Never, and I've never heard of it happening to anyone else. That's what these cable runs are for—to allow the animals freedom to run and play."

"Well, it's a miracle he's still alive. He must have done it moments before you walked out."

After a couple of hours, the vet left, giving us instructions that would keep us busy for the rest of the night. We set up camp outside around Zamba, since the doctor thought it best not to move him. Sundown brought hot Santa Ana breezes, drifting in from the high desert. The stars were brilliant, the night balmy.

Neighbors and friends had come from miles around to help in any way they could. These were people who had known Zamba since he was a baby. They came with blankets, fruit, all kinds of food. They had automatically planned on staying for the night, or even for a week, if necessary. There were a lot of tears shed that night.

We all took turns keeping the fire going, and the men assisted me in turning Zamba every half hour to prevent the buildup of fluid in his peritoneal cavity. I checked constantly to see that the intravenous needle hadn't slipped out of the vein.

As the evening wore on, a circle of people formed around the fire. Some of the kids got sleepy and gently cuddled up to Zamba for warmth. We watched closely so they wouldn't disturb him, but we thought it might be a good idea for them to have contact with him. Zamba loved kids.

Zamba slept peacefully most of the night, but I kept waking him up to see if he was okay. I've never been as happy to hear anything as I was to hear him moan. What rapture to my ears! I petted him and stroked his head and kept talking to him, reassuring him of all the good things to come.

It was only at that moment that I thought about the movie and our trip to Africa. I had just agreed to make the trip of my life with my Zamba, but at that very moment we had almost lost him. I was humbled by the experience and said a few thankful prayers that night.

Morning found him staggering, trying to get up. A couple of the men and I supported his weight, and we were finally able to get his legs underneath him. Then, like a drunken sailor, he started to walk. He was headed for the oak tree, and we turned him just in time to keep him from hitting his head.

For the rest of that day, he stood up periodically, walked in a tight circle for a bit, then collapsed and slept for a while. By the day's end, we had him in the kitchen, one of his favorite spots. He loved to lie on the cold stone floor and smell the cooking. It looked as though he was out of danger and well on the way to recovery.

Early in the morning of the third day, I got up to see how Zamba was doing. He lay sprawled in a deep sleep against the wall in the kitchen, and I crept along quietly so as not to wake him. But I knocked over a cup when I was making the coffee, and the noise woke him up.

"Morning, Zam. Did you have a nice rest?" I asked.

He responded by yawning and stretching, and then proceeded to come to me. But he walked right into the cabinet next to me, banging his head on the door.

Strange, I thought. I stepped around behind him and called again.

"Come on, boy, over here." He turned a quarter-turn and headed toward me, but off by about forty-five degrees. Missing me by six feet, he walked right into the wall.

"Oh no! Toni!" I yelled. "Toni!"

She appeared in the hall. "What's wrong?" she asked.

"I think Zamba's blind!!"

The vet confirmed my fears: Zamba was totally blind. He explained that when the chain had closed off Zamba's air passage, the optic nerves had also been squeezed. He said that this was not uncommon in this type of accident.

"Will he ever see again?" I asked, brushing my hand over Zamba's eyes.

"He could—one never knows. It depends on the severity of the injury."

"Well, it was pretty severe, wouldn't you say?" I asked him.

"Yes, but that massive mane helped offset some of the damage. Only time will tell."

"How much time? I need to tell the studio something. I can't let them continue to think the production will go on, when . . ." I couldn't find the words.

"How soon will you have to leave?" the vet asked.

"In about six weeks."

The vet put his hand on my shoulder, "Ralph, we'll know something in three. Can you wait before you talk to the studio?"

I looked at Toni, then at Zamba. Would it be fair? Here they were basing an entire film on my lion, hiring locals and setting up travel arrangements for a huge production company. But I knew Zamba. He was strong, and his whole history was one of survival. He'd survived in the wild as a cub, he'd survived the freak blizzard at the ranch; I wasn't going to doubt his strength now.

"Yeah, we can wait," I said, stroking Zamba's mane. "No problem."

Toni and I massaged Zamba's throat every few hours, day after day, and administered his medicine religiously. Although he seemed to be getting stronger, we noticed no improvement in his vision. Most mornings we would lead him out into the field alongside the house, where he would "look" off into the distance. I thought, over and over during those days, how wonderful he was. What an extraordinary capacity animals have to accept their problems! No moaning, no self-pity—just acceptance and quiet dignity.

He did need our help, though. We learned quickly that a "harrumph!" from Zamba meant that he had to visit his tree. I would put a canvas harness around his chest, similar to those used for seeing-eye dogs. Then, with Zamba pressing hard against my leg, he and I would walk outside. After a few days, I didn't even need to use a harness. If he was touching my leg, that was sufficient for him to feel secure.

We would take long walks up the slope. For the most part, Zamba's gait was smooth and graceful; occasionally he would stumble, but then only for a moment. At the top, Zamba would first sit on his haunches and appear to gaze off into the distance, and then he'd lie down in the soft green of the field.

I would comb his mane with my fingers. I must have said that I was sorry a thousand times, but each time hurt as much as the first. He was so forgiving, never questioning, and never hesitating in his love for me. To have his kind of peace of mind, to accept everything without complaint—I struggled to learn those things that came so naturally to him. He was born, like his fathers and forefathers, to turn the negatives into positives. We shared the same environment, the same world, he and I, and yet he felt a different wind blowing. The smell of the great outdoors was designed for his pleasure only. He saw everything with his great eyes, and the roar of his voice answered questions we would never have known to ask.

Why is it that animals have attained such perfection in their existence, while man has never known anything even approaching such tranquillity? I have always believed that animals listen to one perfect voice—nature's voice—and do as it bids them. We, on the other hand, listen only to ourselves, and we do as we please. Our ego, our pride, is our instructor, and that force is so powerful that it can make us ignore the reality presented to us by our intellects, and by common sense. It forces us to live superficially, driven by personality, not by character.

Zamba and I spent a lot of quiet time together during those

weeks on the slope. Zamba would lie with his toes touching mine, as he always did in bed. It was his way of knowing whether I was leaving—it was clear to us both that he didn't want to be left alone. I lay on the grass opposite him, looking into those huge, unseeing eyes. I wanted so badly for him to see again, for the energy and forces of his nature to restore his sight. I thought that by connecting our powers we could, together, make that happen. I've always believed that the mind rules the physical body, and that if only we can penetrate to our subconscious, we can tell our bodies to heal.

One evening I went to bring Zamba in from the field. As I went, I thought about a game we used to play. I would get down really low and make a clicking noise with my tongue. This was his signal to "act" like a lion. He would lie in wait for me, ears flat, chin on the ground, tail twitching, body tense. Then I would break into a run, and he would explode after me in an all-out race. Leaping high on those powerful hind legs, he would pounce on me, knocking me flat, licking my face like a giant, overgrown puppy. It had been good fun. I took a deep breath.

"At least he's still alive," I murmured to myself.

As I walked toward him, I noticed that his head was down, his tail was twitching, and his ears were flat. He was stalking me! I could hardly believe what I was seeing. I said a silent prayer, bent low, and made the clicking noise with my tongue. In an instant, Zamba was racing toward me full tilt. I raced away, leaping with joy. He could see again!

He caught me in midair. We hit the ground together, rolling over and over in the soft field. I pulled his great head to me and kissed both his eyes.

"I love you, Zam."

I never did make the call to the studio.

19

Preparing for a long journey always takes a certain amount of organization and planning, even when you're not traveling with lions.

First, we had learned a little bit more about our assignment. It would require three lions to depict all the big cat scenes. Zamba, of course, would play the lead. I chose to take the very best lions in my collection. Tammy, a fabulous four-hundred-pound lioness, was one of the most loving lions I've known. She was gorgeous, too—she had the most striking face I have ever seen, in all the lions I've known, in the wild or in captivity. It was as though her features were painted on by the Almighty Himself. The acting she had to perform would be difficult, but I knew she could do it.

We would also be taking Zamba Jr. He was fifty pounds lighter than Zamba, but he could double for the star in certain shots, and he could also play another lion. He was a talented actor, skilled enough to show all the savagery a lion can muster one minute, and then turn into a mild pussycat the next. I felt confident that I was going to Africa with the best animals for the roles.

There was a lot to be done to prepare for the trip. A month before we left, we had put the lions' travel cages into their compound so they would get accustomed to them. I instructed my trainers to feed the lions inside the cages and to use them as sleeping quarters. By the time we were ready to go, the lions felt completely at home in them.

The lions were ready for the trip—was I? The studio had told us to plan on being gone for at least six months, and although we didn't know it then, we would end up being there for more than a year. I felt confident that the business would run well in my absence—the people I had put in charge knew what to do. It was harder to leave Toni, even though we had known each other only a few months. It didn't seem realistic to ask her to wait for me—we just didn't know each other well enough. So, with tears, we parted ways.

The morning of the departure we fed the lions a light breakfast. They were going to be caged for about fourteen hours, and I didn't want them to carry full stomachs when they couldn't move around much. We were going to have to remain in England overnight, filling out documentation and loading equipment, so I had made arrangements with the London Royal Society for the Prevention of Cruelty to Animals (RSPCA) to provide an area where the lions could exercise and have a proper meal.

After they'd eaten breakfast, we loaded all three of them and headed for LAX. We were greeted there by an American Society for the Prevention of Cruelty to Animals officer, who weighed the cats: Zamba came in at 528 pounds, Junior at 480, and Tammy at 350 pounds.

"I need the health certificate on each lion, and their tranquilizer report," said the health official at the animal control office. I looked questioningly at him as I handed over the health papers. "You did tranquilize them for the journey, didn't you?" he asked.

"No, I never do. It's too dangerous," I said.

The official looked at me with a disbelieving expression. "Well, we'll have to do it here. They have to be tranquilized for travel," he insisted. "They could panic and break out of their crates."

He gestured to his assistant to bring the tranquilizers.

He was right in one respect: many zoo-raised, wild, or even highly excitable domestic animals (like racehorses) did need to be tranquilized for travel, lest they injure themselves or others trying to escape unfamiliar surroundings. But he needed to understand that my lions were different.

"With all due respect, sir, lions can hallucinate under a drug and be uncontrollable—just like a person. It's better that they know what's going on. I'm afraid the drug could cause a reaction that would make them unmanageable, or even kill them," I said. "These lions were brought up in a human environment, and have been subjected to all of the noises, smells, and activities that they're likely to encounter on this trip. They understand what's going on. The tranquilizer you use is for hyperactive, zoo-raised, or wild animals. These lions are different. They're not seeing the world for the first time; they live in it."

The officer was getting upset. He didn't like me challenging his authority.

"Look, I don't care what you say. A lion is a lion. Either we tranquilize them, or they don't fly." We spent hours trying to convince him and the other animal control people that our lions were safer without any drugs. Finally the studio had to step in and convince them to let us go, once we had signed a waiver of responsibility.

I couldn't ride with them in the hold on the first leg of the journey, but when we got to London I was allowed to help unload them and to take them to the RSPCA. As promised, we were given a special holding area so they could get some exercise. We opened the cage doors, and the lions filed out into their temporary home, greeting us with rubs and moans, and then casually peeing on the nearest tree. They had a good meal and full night's sleep before we loaded them into the plane the next morning. We had no trouble with the RSPCA regarding tranquilization. After the difficulty in Los Angeles, the studio had called ahead and made arrangements.

The studio had hired a private DC-6, a huge plane that could carry up to eighty passengers. It was enormous inside, especially because practically all of the plane's infrastructure had been removed. All the seats had been removed except two: one for my assistant, Kellen, and one for me. The toilet remained; otherwise the whole plane was practically empty. The studio's equipment—props, cameras, film, etc.—took up a small amount of space in the back of the plane, and we had the freedom to wander the wide open space that was left. I never figured out why they had hired such an enormous plane for three measly lions, but so be it.

The lions were the last thing loaded onto the plane; large forklifts lifted their cages one by one, and the cages were then strapped down and bolted for security. I positioned the cages so that the lions could see me and Kellen at all times.

Before takeoff, the captain, copilot, and steward came over and introduced themselves. They were the only other people on board.

"They're sure big!" the copilot exclaimed. "I never realized just how big they were until now. Seeing them up close really brings it home."

The captain reminded us to be sure the cages were securely locked. We assured him that they were.

At takeoff, we talked to the cats, reaching our hands into the cages and stroking them to give them a feeling of security. Without the plane's infrastructure, the motors were deafening. When we settled at our cruising altitude, the roar subsided to a steady hum. The lions barely reacted. By the time we were in the air, Zamba was already lying down resting comfortably. The other two were licking their fur.

Kellen and I unfastened our seat belts and walked around the plane. We could have set up a basketball court, with room to spare. Brian, the steward, came out with some drinks and snacks. He couldn't take his eyes off the lions.

"They are the most beautiful creatures I have ever seen," he remarked. "And they seem so docile."

I smiled. "Well, they are. Beautiful and docile."

Zamba yawned, and Brian tripped as he was leaving, almost spilling his tray of drinks and food. "Sorry," he said, shaking his head.

About two hours into the flight, the captain invited us into the cockpit where he explained all the dials, controls, and principles of flight. Flying at about twenty thousand feet, we had crossed over Italy and the Mediterranean, and were now flying over Egypt. We were headed due south for East Africa, the beltline of the continent: the equator runs directly through it. The continent of Africa is about three times bigger than the United States. We would stop in Khartoum for fuel, and from there, it would take us about ten hours to reach Nairobi.

I could see the vast stretches of the great Sahara desert below me, and I can't even begin to describe the tremendous feeling of pride and excitement and anticipation I felt as I looked down. I felt as if it really penetrated for the first time—when we got off this plane, Zamba and I would be in Africa together.

The hours droned by. The captain or one of his crew would periodically come out to see how we were doing. The steward brought sandwiches and drinks. Finally the captain pointed out the city of Khartoum in the distance as we started our descent. It was time to gas up.

The plane landed softly despite all the potholes in the runway. We had to park at the far end of the runway as a security measure because the lions were on board. It didn't seem to matter; news of the lions had traveled rapidly, and hordes of people with their camels and goats were running down the runway toward our plane. How they knew we were arriving was a mystery.

We were in for a shock when we opened the doors. Unbearable heat hit our faces like a blast from a furnace, and the temperature in the plane rose in a matter of minutes. The atmosphere was suffocating. Never before had I experienced such heat. The lions stood up and started to breathe heavily. I was worried about Zamba and Zamba Jr.; their manes were so heavy, I was afraid they would suffer heat stroke.

I explained the danger to the captain, and he ordered the doors closed and the air conditioner left on. Kellen stayed behind while I went with the captain to fill out the permits for the cats. We pushed our way through the crowd and headed for the operations building. The heat was stifling, and by the time we arrived we were wringing wet. I wondered how the people around us, wearing their customary turbans and *kanzus*, the long cotton robes worn by Muslim men, could possibly stay cool.

I was fascinated by the camels. They were everywhere, bawling their displeasure at one thing or another. Most of them wore bells, bangles, and bright-colored blankets, and had tufted wool balls swinging from their reins. They all had intricate, painful-looking brands burned into their skin. Some of them were ridden by young children who whipped them with little sticks; others wandered freely, along with small groups of goats.

We signed the documents and headed back to the plane. As intrigued as I was by my surroundings, I was anxious to get back to the lions. The local airport attendants were just finishing filling the gas tanks as we arrived back at the plane. A dozen men in uniforms, the local law enforcement, came onto the field, pushing and shoving the gawkers and their camels in an attempt to get them off the field. It wasn't until the engines started up that the camels bolted and ran off.

We blasted off, circled the city, then set our bearings for Nairobi, Kenya. Soon, it was very hot in the airplane. We took off our shirts when they started dripping with sweat. After we had been airborne about a half hour, I noticed the lions were sweating and breathing hard. I called the captain on the intercom.

"Excuse me, sir," I said. "The lions are really very hot back here."

"Sorry about that. The air conditioner isn't working well enough to cool the whole plane."

I called again half an hour later, but there was no answer other than the one I'd already gotten. By now the lions were drooling, and their skin was sopping wet.

I talked to the pilot a few more times, even discussing the possibility of landing somewhere to cool them off, but between where we were and Nairobi there was no runway big enough to accommodate the plane. He also pointed out that it would still be very hot wherever we landed. "It's best to keep on flying." There was nothing he could do.

I had to do something. Tammy wasn't suffering as much as the other two, but Zamba's and Zamba Jr.'s manes were now drenched. I motioned to Kellen.

"Turn them loose," I said. "Help me open the cage doors."

I got up, fumbled for the keys, and started to unlock the doors.

"Are you crazy? The captain's going to have kittens if he finds

Time for a catnap! Zamba with Ralph and an assistant trainer.

Zamba gets groomed to look his best by Ralph.

Zamba waits patiently for Ralph while on location.

Story time with Zamba and three-year-old Tana.

Ralph gives Zamba the tender touch.

Ralph's arm in the trusted jaws of Zamba.

Ralph, Toni, and Zamba Jr.

Tana at seven with Zamba.

Poster for *Fluffy*.

Shirley Jones plays a tune for Zamba.

Betty White, Mike Connors, an unidentified blind woman, Ralph, and Zamba.

The Helfer family—Toni, Tana, Ralph, and Zamba.

William Holden gets a playful sniff from Zamba as Ralph looks on.

Zamba and Pamela on location for the movie *The Lion*.

Ralph, Cher, Sonny, Toni, and Modoc the elephant.

Ralph sitting on top of Twigga.

Ralph and Gentle Ben.

Ralph surrounded by elephant friends
(left to right) Modoc, Taj, Debbie, and Misty.

out." Kellen stood up. "Ralph—are you sure about this? Hadn't you better tell him first?"

"If I do, he'll say no, and if we don't do something these cats are going to suffer heat exhaustion. Are you going to just stand there or are you going to help?"

We raised the cage doors, and one by one the cats walked out. They were all soaking wet and breathing hard. At the bottom of each cage was a puddle of sweat mixed with the bedding straw, creating a soggy mess. The cats gave us their usual greeting by rubbing against us. They peed against the wall and proceeded to explore the whole plane, smelling and rubbing every surface, and finally settled down where the passenger air conditioner blowers were the most powerful.

We pointed the blowers at the lions and wiped them down with some paper towels from the toilet. A bit of combing helped the air to circulate and dry out their fur. Then we joined them stretched out on the cabin floor to relax under the blowers. They closed their eyes and let the air blow across their faces. Within an hour much of their sweat had dried off.

Once they were a little more comfortable, each took a window, lying down and watching the clouds drift by. Tammy wanted to be with Zamba, so she climbed up and lay across him to see what he was seeing. It was a wonderful, awe-inspiring moment, seeing them so calm, so interested in the cloud formations. They didn't know they were twenty thousand feet up in the air, traveling at more than three hundred miles an hour. They didn't know that the clouds were made of water and no, you couldn't walk on them.

I stroked Zamba's mane. He rolled over into my lap and closed his eyes, totally contented. Was it his lack of awareness that made his purity of heart possible? I was deliberating the point when the cabin door opened. I bolted from my stupor.

"Oh boy!" murmured Kellen as he jumped up, moving to head off Brian coming out of the cockpit.

"I brought you some chow and—holy shit!" The man's mouth hung open. Kellen grabbed the tray just as it started to fall. "Oh my God. Are you both crazy?"

He stood there in total shock, not knowing what to do or where to go. Kellen managed to close the door behind him before the others found out.

"Oh shit! Oh shit!" His breathing was heavy and uneven.

I hurried over to him, grabbed his arm, and led him over to our seats. "Here, sit down, relax. They're not going to hurt you."

"What in the hell are you guys doing? You're both mad. We'll all be killed!"

"They'll only kill you if we're not happy with the food," cracked Kellen. His dry humor didn't help.

"No really, it's okay, it's totally safe. Please don't worry." I comforted the man, shooting daggers at Kellen.

Poor Brian looked like someone who had just been thrown into ice water. Zamba was annoyed that I had disturbed him when I jumped up and was looking for another comfy place to lie down, but Tammy was curious about our guest. Kellen was supporting Brian's weight as best he could, but as Tammy walked toward him, Brian's legs gave way again and he slid down the wall. Tammy came over and rubbed against him, knocking his cap off.

"Go ahead, pet her," I said. The man was useless. Kellen lifted Brian's hand, put it on Tammy's back, and moved it for him. He just gazed straight ahead. Tammy eventually flopped down beside them, head next to Brian's legs, and dozed off. As Brian gradually regained his composure, life came back into his body. His hand started to function on its own.

"My God. Oh my God," was all he could say.

A half hour passed before he had gathered his wits completely. The captain's buzzer sounded.

"Brian, where you? How about some coffee?

"Ah. Yes. Yes, sir, right away. Coming right up, sir."

He slowly got up and slid out from under Tammy's body, not wanting to wake her.

"Don't say anything about the lions."

"Not a problem, sir, not a problem."

He carefully slid through the door into the cockpit so as not to alert the others.

We had just settled down to a bit of sleep when we heard a loud commotion coming from the cockpit.

"They *what?*"

"You *what?* You're kidding me."

A loud discussion followed, and while I couldn't hear it all, I did hear words like "killer" and "savage attack." After a little while, the door opened slightly, and we could see part of the captain's face as he peered out into the coach area. Brian was in the background, and I could hear him valiantly trying to tell the boss how wonderful the cats were.

"What in the hell do you think you're doing? You're breaking every rule in the book. Put them back in their cages, *now!*"

Kellen and his dry sense of humor again. "Don't worry, sir, they just had lunch. Besides, I used to fly a Piper Cub."

I tried to calm the captain down.

"Look, sir—these lions are very special. They're going to be working with a small girl in the movie we're going to do."

He was unmoved. So Kellen and I got up and did every possible thing we could with the lions to prove to the captain how safe they were. We rode them, put our hands in their mouths, pulled their tails, kissed them, though they made it clear that they'd rather be sleeping. It took an hour for the captain to be convinced to come into the coach cabin.

But by the time we were in sight of the Nairobi airport, everybody on board had met the lions. The pilot and copilot were taking turns flying the plane so they could take pictures with the copilot's little Kodak camera to prove it had happened. They wouldn't rest until we had promised them all a visit to the set to see the film being made. After a final lick from Zamba for the captain's face, all the cats went back in their cages. We roared down the runway to a perfect landing.

20

Coming to Africa had a profound effect on both Zamba and me. He was returning home to his birthplace, and a place where he had almost died, and I was finally seeing a place that I had dreamed about all my life. In a way, I felt that I was also coming home. I couldn't explain the feeling; I just knew that I had real ties to this place.

A representative from the production company assisted with the paperwork at the airport. Once the animal control officer had checked the health of the lions by looking at them through their cages (he wasn't about to take them out), he released them to us. They were loaded, still in their cages, onto a cart and wheeled into the parking lot where hundreds of people had gathered. A huge uproar greeted us as we made our way through the crowd toward the two vehicles waiting for us.

The bigger of the two vehicles had two large built-in cages in the back. We put leads on Zamba Jr. and Tammy and walked them over to the truck. We jumped them up on the trucks and into their new transport cages. Kellen settled down in the back of the truck to keep watch. When they saw the lions, the crowd retreated a good ten yards, and not a few people ran clear across the parking lot, tripping over one another, yelling and screaming. It may seem naïve, but it had never occurred to me that African people would react in such a way. I later learned that many of them had never actually seen a lion before.

A brand new Land Rover was parked nearby.

"This is for you and Zamba, a gift from the production company," said the rep.

Painted on the side was a beautiful portrait of Zamba, with the words "THE LION" underneath. I was told it was the work of one of the best artists in Kenya. It was a wonderful welcome.

As I was admiring the Rover, a tall African man dressed in traditional attire walked toward us. He wore a bright red *shuku*, or wrap, that covered most of his body, with the end tucked into his belt. His earlobes hung nearly to his shoulders and were decorated with beaded earrings, and he wore his hair in long, thin red braids. (Masai warriors groom their hair with a mixture of goat fat, water, and mud from the banks of the local river. The result is a rich reddish color.) A sizable knife was secured in a skin sheath hanging from a leather belt, and his shoes were obviously cut from car tires. Across his muscular chest were three strings of colored beads: red, white, and black.

In any other place he would have stood out, but here he was merely dressed in his tribal garb. A quick look into the crowd showed others in similar dress.

"*Sopa*," he said, as he extended his hand in greeting.

I was impressed immediately by the aura of power and strength he conveyed, offset by his gentle smile.

"*Sopa*," I responded, not knowing what it meant, but it just seemed natural to answer back.

He smiled.

"Ralph, this is your driver," the production rep said. "He will be available to you for your stay here. He is a moran, a warrior of the Masai tribe."

"Well, okay. Glad to have you on board," I said as we shook hands. "What is your name? "

"My name is very difficult for you *mzungu* to say. Most of my friends just call me Masai." *Mzungu* means "white people."

"Nice to know you. Come on over and give me a hand, Masai."

If he was going to be driving us, he'd be spending a lot of time around lions. I figured that now would be as good a time as ever to see how he handled himself in their presence.

We went over and lifted Zamba's cage door together. As Zamba came out, I put a loop of chain around his neck and headed for the Rover. Masai went ahead and opened the door for Zamba to hop in.

Zamba stopped at the Rover, got his nostrils full of that new car aroma, and then paused to check out Masai. Finally he gave his approval by jumping aboard. We saw the rear end of the Rover get a couple of inches closer to the ground.

"Better make a note to put some heavy-duty shocks back there," I said.

"For sure," said Masai.

I was impressed by the way Masai had stood his ground while Zamba gave him the once-over. Zamba's gaze can be very penetrating, and could make people flee the scene in a hurry. Looking over my shoulder at the crowd of people watching from afar, I turned back to Masai.

"Aren't you afraid of the lion?" I asked.

"Yes," he answered.

"But you didn't move?"

"I am Masai."

"Oh," I said.

The production rep spoke up. "We'd best be going."

The horde of people waved their good-byes and chanted, *"Simba! Simba! Simba!"* as we headed into the countryside. It means "lion."

The rep sat up front with Masai. I kept Zamba company in the back. I opened the hatch in the roof so Zamba could stick his head out. Even when he was sitting down, his head stuck up a good two feet above the roof. People walking on the edge of the road looked in disbelief, and more than one person tripped over his own feet because he couldn't believe his eyes.

Zamba was thrilled. The wind was blowing his mane; he was taking in the sights. I was enjoying myself as well. Not ten minutes out of the airport I saw a sign that said RHINO CROSSING and yet in the near distance I saw what appeared to be the buildings of Nairobi, the capital of Kenya. Apparently the city was built very close to the bush.

In just fifteen minutes we were out of the town and into the country, and it was extraordinarily beautiful. Roadside stands selling mangos, oranges, bananas, and all kinds of vegetables slowly disappeared, and in their place, animals started to appear— ostriches, zebras, impalas, gazelles, as well as a few giraffes in the distance and some antelopes. It wasn't long before the road turned rough and dusty, riddled with potholes.

Within the hour, Zamba had gotten used to the bumping and had settled in quite well. He had given up on looking around and was sleeping away. I reached over and ruffled his mane. "Hey, Zam, you're home, boy." For my sentimentality, I got a throaty "aggh!" and a tail whip across my chest.

We drove north. Two hours later, we arrived in Nanyuki, a small settlement located at the base of the looming and majestic Mount

Kenya, its two peaks capped with snow. Another fifteen minutes brought us to the magnificent and world famous Mount Kenya Safari Club, which was owned by actor William Holden and his business partners. This was to be our home for the duration of the filming.

A large throng of people was gathered at the entrance, awaiting our arrival. The staff of the club, the studio crew, and a host of onlookers were all there to greet the four-legged star. I lowered the back door, helped Zamba jump out, and walked him over to a spacious lawn, in front of a shimmering swimming pool. Off in the near distance stood the majestic and snowcapped Mount Kenya, seventeen thousand feet tall. Masai was at my side.

I was honored when the star of the movie, Bill Holden, appeared to welcome us to the club. So did the other notables in the cast: Trevor Howard, the Parisian model and actress Capucine, and our friend Pamela Franklin, the child actress. The director and producer, along with most of the crew, were there as well.

A woman approached us. She had rusty red hair that blew against her pale, slightly freckled face. Her low voice was arresting; she sounded British, but the rhythm of her speech was slightly different—I was to find out that she was a third-generation Kenyan. She smiled a welcome to me; the smile was incredibly warm and lit her entire face.

"Hi. I'm Pippa," she said, extending her hand.

"Hi, there," I said. "I'm Ralph."

"I've never touched a lion before." Another warm, hopeful smile crossed her face.

"Neither had I—once."

"*Pole?*" she said. It means "Sorry?"

"Never mind."

I told her to approach Zamba just behind me. The crew photographer snapped a picture. That opened a floodgate. "Oh! Please, can I?" and "Me, too?" until most of the group had had their pictures taken in Africa with their arm around a lion.

I simply couldn't take my eyes off this exciting redhead. And it was mutual. During the time that we were in Africa, Pippa and I were to become inseparable. In my eyes, she was the perfect woman to show me Africa—for me, she *was* Africa. She would share her love for this great country with me, show me things I had never even imagined, and teach me as much Swahili as I could learn. But I didn't know that yet.

When the other lions arrived in the slower truck, we were escorted to a spot below the pool, close to the edge of the forest, a place that we would later dub the Lions' Den. I had plans sent ahead for the construction, but I was amazed by the creativity that had been lavished on the design. The entire facility was dressed in natural materials, and looked as if it had been there for years. It sat near a freshwater river that cascaded down through the forest from Mount Kenya.

The den itself consisted of a four-room African *shamba,* or house. The main entrance leading into the building was made of cedar and bamboo. Its top was arched and covered with a thick layer of elephant grass.

Inside there were three lion "apartments" fashioned after a Masai *manyatta,* or village. Each room had a strong, heavy bed made of Meru oak, four feet off the ground and substantial enough to hold a lion's weight comfortably. The fourth room held all the equipment needed to handle the lions. Along one wall hung a variety of chains, canes, leads, clips, and other paraphernalia. Another wall held an array of medicines, brushes, combs, special devices, tranquilizer guns—not that we'd be needing them!—and accessories.

All the rooms opened out into the house's main area. A six-inch-thick teakwood chopping block stood on an counter-height island in the middle. All the meals were prepared here with special vitamins and minerals at hand to work into the meat. The compound's walls were made of a mixture of cow dung and mud plastered over six-gauge chain link. The roof was covered with woven swamp reed thatching, which would keep the compound cool at all times but was still thick enough to stop any rain from seeping through. Water was piped in twenty-four hours a day from the freshwater springs coming off Mount Kenya.

A fenced yard surrounded the house so the lions could lounge, relax, or exercise when it was cool enough to be outside. We also used it as a training area. I later learned that the large tree in the center of the compound, and one that the lions loved to use to sharpen their claws, was a Mugumo tree. I came to understand that it was a very spiritual tree, and one that many of the local people came to pray under. It was big enough to sustain the damage from the lions' huge claws, and the locals were happy to lend use of the tree, as lions are highly respected in all of East Africa.

This was surely a palace fit for the King of Beasts.

I stayed nearby, in a luxurious suite adjoining the main hotel, just over a grass rise from the Lions' Den. The view was spectacular. The grounds of the club were beautifully landscaped and blended in with the nearby mountain forest. Jacaranda trees with their vivid purple flowers, Cape chestnut, acacia, and giant fig were just a few of the trees that graced the grounds. In the near distance, the glorious peak of Mount Kenya rose majestically.

I was amazed to find that herds of elephants, buffaloes, impalas, water bucks, and lions were among the many species that frequented the forest just a few yards away. I assumed that the small fence that bordered the grounds was a sufficient barrier to keep the forest on that side and the club on the other. I was proven wrong on numerous occasions.

We put each lion into his or her own room. They explored the rooms thoroughly, sniffing and smelling the different woods, opening their mouths to more fully appreciate all these new smells. The house was a hit.

That first night, I slept in the compound with Zamba. I was afraid he would be frightened and need someone to hold his paw. Maybe I babied him too much, but he meant everything to me, and I wanted his first night in this special place to be special.

Early the next morning, I was repairing some of our equipment that had been damaged during the trip. One of the Askaris, our guards, came in with a man.

"This is Njoka. He wants to work for you."

He was of the Kikuyu tribe, and had a slight build, light-colored skin, and piercing dark eyes, although he kept them cast down as I spoke to him.

"Aren't you afraid to work with the lions?" I asked.

"Yes, sir."

"How will you be able to function?"

"Yes, sir."

"What is your name?"

"Yes, sir."

It didn't take but a minute to realize that he didn't speak any English.

"Sorry," I said. "No English, no job."

The Askari translated for Njoka, who said, with great effort, "I . . . speak you Swahili. Then we understand. You in Africa now. Okay. Okay?"

He was right, I thought. I should learn a bit of Swahili, and at the same time he'll learn a bit of English.

"Okay. We'll give it a go. How do I say okay?" I asked the Askari.

"*Sawa sawa*," he said.

"*Sawa sawa*," I said to Njoka.

He smiled, then went over and sat on a stool. I guess he figured to start right that minute. The guard left. I put Njoka to work cutting up meat and preparing the lion food. Njoka was to become a good friend, one I could always count on. I also did learn quite a bit of Swahili. If he could teach me a language, I guess that means he was a pretty good teacher.

Every day at the club was a celebration of life. It took all my self-control not to run the lawns with Zam, shouting out my happiness at all the wonders around me. The grounds of the club were truly magical, filled with running streams, flowers, plants, and trees. And the animals! The variety in the bird life alone was astounding: marabou storks, egrets, kiwis, kites, Egyptian geese, and a Sari crane that the staff told me had been there for years. It had been attacked by a leopard once and survived, and another time by a baboon. One wing was damaged, but the bird still strutted its stuff throughout the grounds.

About four o'clock each day, the bird man came to feed the birds. An old man, he carried a satchel filled with bird food over one shoulder. Not just seed, but cut-up fruit as well: mangoes, apples, oranges, grapes, and lots of pawpaw. When the birds saw him coming, they would swoop down from the trees and rooftops, landing at his feet. Many of the birds were marabou storks, the largest birds in Africa, with six-foot wingspans. They would launch themselves off the tops of the giant trees and glide across the grounds, coming in for landing like a 747. As they approached the ground, their feet touched down with an occasional hop, just like the wheels of a plane, before bringing them to a halt just inches from the bird man. It was something to see.

If we weren't working on the set, every day at four o'clock, Zamba would strain against his lead to go see the birds. He never tried to chase them, but he was definitely fascinated by the way they flew and landed. Many bits of food landed within a few feet of him, and the birds picked it up and ate it unconcernedly; they didn't seem to mind his being there and treated him just like a person.

The division between nature and the club wasn't always clear. One night some of the actors and crew were having drinks and telling stories when, suddenly, Kellen burst through the door.

"LION! LION!" He was yelling and out of breath. I could see the color had drained from his face. Capucine went to get him some water, while Bill Holden and I tried to settle him down.

"Kellen, calm down. What happened?" I asked.

"I was walking down to check the lions for the night, and I saw Zamba standing on the trail. I thought he had gotten out of his room somehow, so I chastised him. 'What are you doing? Get back inside right now! You hear me?'"

"And?" I waited, a little nervous.

"Well, he ran back toward the compound, and then instead of going inside, he ran off into the jungle!"

Capucine came back with the water.

"I went into the compound to get his lead so I could take him back and—and there was Zamba, in his room! It wasn't Zamba out there at all! It was some other wild lion I had been yelling at! Man, I don't think I touched the ground getting back up here."

We found out later that a big male had been coming in from the forest to woo Tammy. And we never stopped teasing Kellen, all the time we were in Kenya.

The club staff were also some of the nicest people I have ever known. Many had been there since its inception and treated us like guests in their house.

I made special friends with a young Indian boy named Vinod, or Vinny, as he liked to be called. He ran the shortwave radio on the set, and it was from him that I first heard the nickname I'd been given by the locals: Bwana Simba, the boss of the lions.

"You're Zamba's boss?" he asked.

I laughed. "Well, sometimes—sometimes he's the boss."

"Can I meet him when he's not too busy?"

"You mean, like make an appointment?"

"I don't want to interfere with his schedule."

I put my arm on Vinny's shoulder. "Zamba would be more then happy to meet you," I said. I arranged for an "appointment" the following day. All three of us became fast friends. Vinny was always the first to offer his help, and in return I let him come to the lion house and get to know the cats.

It was also an honor to meet and get to know Jacob, one of the managers at the club. He was second in charge and always available to greet visitors. He remains one of the most charismatic men I have ever met. His smile was infectious, and when you were away, it was his energy that brought you back. In all the years I was to frequent the club, he was always there to smile and embrace anyone coming in from a long safari or on arriving from far-off places. You always felt that he genuinely cared about your well-being, and when he was talking to you, he conveyed the impression that you were the most important thing in his life.

Our life at the club fell into a lovely routine. Every morning, if the weather was good and we weren't working on the movie, I would take Zamba out for his brushing and grooming. Sometimes Masai would join me; he loved to help with the grooming. At least thirty children would be waiting patiently on the club lawn in hopes that the breeze would blow the hair in their direction. As I brushed his mane, I pulled the hair apart so there would be enough for everybody. It seemed like the least I could do—where else could they possibly get hair from a lion's mane?

Many of the children had been sent to bring some home for their fathers. A piece of lion hair symbolized good times, health, and above all, strength. Both the children and the adults would weave it into their own hair. Some of the elders tied it around their stretched earlobes. I am sure many pieces were sold. When a good breeze would blow, it was pure excitement, with all the kids screaming and yelling and scrambling to catch Zamba's hair.

Once, while the children were enjoying themselves, something totally bizarre happened. The sun, which had been bright and hot, began to lose its glow. There were no clouds in the sky, but something was clearly happening. I heard a low, ominous, vibrating sound, and saw what appeared to be a tornado descending on the club: a big, powerful black cloud, spinning like a top, its long, snakelike arm swaying to and fro and coming closer and closer.

As the sky darkened, the children screamed and ran for cover. I watched as the cloud came directly overhead, then slowly began to descend like a giant helicopter. It was then that I realized it wasn't a tornado at all but a swarm of locusts! Millions of them. I had never seen anything like it. I knew very little about locusts, other than that some invade every twenty years.

I quickly ran Zamba into the nearest doorway, which happened to be the bar. I figured the locusts couldn't hurt him, but I didn't want him to panic. He didn't, but the bartender inside, who was busy preparing the afternoon buffet snacks, jumped over the bar at the sight of him, knocking over the table of hors d'oeuvres that he was preparing.

"*Pole,*" I said.

I would never have imagined how threatening a locust swarm can be. The humming drone was ear-splitting and inescapable as the dark cloud slowly settled on the club. Millions upon millions of huge locusts landed everywhere, eating all the vegetation in sight. These were not little grasshoppers—some were as long as four inches! Drawn outside to look, I was covered in seconds.

I remembered reading that the locust plague was an awesome spectacle and one of the most feared pestilences of the ancient world. The average locust can consume many times its own weight every day, and a swarm, an army of insects numbering in the hundreds of millions per square mile, can amass in minutes. The garden, full of corn, beans, lettuce, squash, and many other vegetables, was inundated, as well as certain other bushes and flowering plants. The roadway was covered with them, inches deep. A truck coming down the road, now slippery with locusts, careened off into a ditch.

All of a sudden, the club's staff burst out of every door: waiters, kitchen help, and drivers, all running outside with bags. They collected the locusts as fast as they could, stuffing them in every conceivable place. The children joined in.

For a half hour the club was completely covered in locusts, and then, as though responding to some signal unheard by us, they took their loud, vibrating sound off into the sky. Within moments, everything was back to normal, except the decimated foliage they'd left behind. The sky was clear again, as if they'd never been there. One little boy said, "They gave us back our sun."

After that, everywhere you went, the Africans were eating locusts—fried, boiled, roasted. Children were running around with them sticking out of their mouths, a foot here, a head there. I tasted some. Not bad!

21

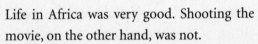Life in Africa was very good. Shooting the movie, on the other hand, was not.

While we were there, Kenya was inundated with the worst rains in thirty years. Rivers overflowed their banks in all parts of the country, and the earth could hold no more water. Villages were swept away, and many lives were lost. The black cotton murram roads were as slippery as grease, and travel became near impossible.

The shoot was supposed to take six months, but it would be a year before we were back in the States. Day after day, the production was canceled because no one could get to the location, and even if we had gotten there successfully, the heavy downpour made it impossible to film. The lions stayed warm and calm either in their "house" or in their accommodations on location. When the sun would burst through, we'd quickly call everybody to duty to take advantage of the rare moment of light.

Costs mounted, and the studio tried over and over to cancel the production, but there was already a lot invested, and the producers were tenacious, so they focused on ways to get the shots and get out. The production company built a soundstage at the club, which included sets where the majority of the scenes were to be shot, so those could be done inside. It was a pleasure to shoot in a warm, comfortable environment, but it wasn't all easy going. The drumming of the rain reverberated throughout the makeshift studio and caused the sound man an inordinate amount of problems. Much of the dialogue had to be dubbed later.

The bright side of losing so many shooting days was that it gave me a great deal of time to spend with Pippa. My relationship with her was unlike that with any woman I had known before her. Her confidence and humor made it possible for us to spend seemingly endless amounts of time together. We spent a great deal of time during those rainy days getting to know the cast and crew.

As I had hoped, Zamba and young Pam became fast friends. She rode on his back, helped to wash him down before a scene, and would brush his drying mane for hours. He loved to put his head on her lap (but for just a short time; it would quickly become too heavy for her), and to pop balloons that she tossed for him.

It was on *The Lion* that I had the great pleasure of working with and getting to know Trevor Howard, one of the great actors of our time, perhaps best known for David Lean's *Brief Encounter*, or for his role in *The Third Man*. He was a wonderful person (as well as a great actor, no matter what shenanigans we'd been up to the night before), and we became good friends while visiting the local pubs or the many private homes that welcomed him with open arms.

It was Trevor Howard who introduced me and Pippa to the Treetops, in the heart of Aberdare National Park. It was one of his favorite places, a great place to stay overnight and see the various exotic animals come to the waterhole to drink and lick the salt that had permeated the ground around it. There were decks, balconies, and lounges covering every angle, so you could "talk to the animals" while enjoying a rather strong drink from the bar.

Capucine (we called her Cap) was often there as well. She was a model from France who had turned her hand to acting (you might know her from *What's New, Pussycat?*), and a truly lovely lady—inside and out. Her beauty was stunning, but that wasn't what impressed me most—in all those days of shooting, with all the setbacks we encountered, she stayed compassionate and warm, and despite the weather, she never lost her temper or succumbed to depression, like others on the set.

Weather wasn't the only thing holding us back. One day, I was walking Zamba on the club lawn when I heard a commotion at the main entrance. A team of Askari guards were standing in formation by the main entrance. A tall man who appeared to be their captain was talking in Swahili to Jacob.

"What's happening, Jacob, why all the military?"

"It's the Mau Mau again. They just killed a white family over on the Laikipia road. It was pretty brutal—they skinned their children and hung them on the wall."

"That's horrible. Why? What had the whites done?"

"Those particular whites, probably nothing, but this war has been going on for some time.

"How did it start?"

"A tribe known in this area was unhappy with some of its clansmen dealing with the British, so a fight broke out, and that turned into a bloody war. Then the British got into it. But now the British have decided to pull out of Kenya and give it back to the Kenyans, and there's now some unrest about the transition."

The Mau Mau were part of a Kenyan independence movement fighting the British colonial presence in Africa.

"Will the British pull-out stop the war?"

"I think so. We all want it to go away."

The captain sent his men to different areas of the club. Jacob took me by the arm and quietly said, "Ralph, be careful with Zamba."

"Why?"

"There are rumors that some of the Mau Mau might try to stop the production. They could do anything."

"Like what?"

"Well, just keep an eye on him. We've stationed a few Askaris down by the lion house just in case."

I wasn't about to leave Zamba and the other lions' safety up to hired guards, although I had every confidence in the club's ability to take care of us. Kellen, our driver Masai, and I slept in the lion house that night and all of the next week. Quite suddenly, my paradise had turned into a potentially dangerous place, and a sinister quiet fell over the peaceful club.

One night, just after dinner, I walked Cap back to her room. We were chatting when we heard a commotion, then two thuds hit the door, followed by a loud banging. I heard the voice of the Askari captain. When I opened the door, I found him and four of his Askaris swiftly pulling a couple of spears out of the door. They pushed us inside the room and shut the door behind us. Apparently a few Mau Mau had pulled a quick raid on the club, and run off.

The spears were about six feet long, with long, nicely sharpened points. They were quite heavy. Whoever had thrown them must have been either very big or very close. The next morning we were issued .45-caliber pistols, "just in case."

The staff of the club and the studio heads met that night, concerned for everyone's safety and the success of the production. They decided that it would be important to show the African people, especially the Mau Mau, that the British were indeed leaving Kenya, and that this was cause for celebration at the club. They decided to throw a grand party in honor of Kenya getting its independence, Uhuru.

It was planned for the following Saturday. Africans from all over the surrounding Nanyuki and close-by Nyeri areas would be invited. The theme was to say good-bye to the past and welcome in the new.

Pippa joined us as we prepared for the event.

I was curious to know what she thought about the threat of danger. "What do you think?" I asked.

"I can only tell you that the Mau Mau are pretty treacherous. They are capable of anything."

"We'll keep close watch."

On the afternoon of the party, the club was buffed to the hilt. The staff was spit-polished, and the chef had prepared a special menu.

While the sun was still shining, I brought Zamba out on the lawn for a few pictures with the dignitaries: the mayor, some very wealthy conservationists and nearby landowners, the chief of police, and some military big shots. The Askaris watched the crowds very closely. Zamba was feeling good, picking and choosing the people he wanted to be near. Sometimes he'd do that. When someone he didn't like wanted to take a picture with him, he'd turn away. So catty!

When I returned from taking Zamba back to his house, I found that the sun had set, and about thirty or forty small fires had been lit all over the lawns. Small groups of men stood around roasting *mahindi* (corn) and *nyama choma* (meat). It smelled delicious, but the atmosphere was heavy and tense. The men around the fires were segregated; the groups were either all black or all white.

Kellen, a couple of Askari, Pippa, Bill Holden, and some of the crew watched and waited with me. Everybody was jumpy.

We noticed quite a few British solders grouping together. Most were from the army base in Nanyuki. They were easy to pick out, as they had their heads shaved and wore their khaki uniforms. "They're not happy with this, you know," said Bill. "They never did have a good rapport with the locals."

Occasionally we'd hear a whistle and the Askari would rush to different parts of the lawn, breaking up small skirmishes.

"Let's get a drink," suggested Bill.

We headed for the bar, which was packed four deep. A big, tall Brit soldier walked in with a few of his friends, and it was immediately obvious he had had a few too many. The bar was noisy, everybody talking at the same time. The Brit yelled his order to one of two bartenders, who were trying their best to serve everybody.

The bartender acknowledged him but had many other orders ahead of the soldier's. A minute passed. The Brit yelled again for his drink, this time using derogatory language.

"Hey, you get your black ass over here! I'm talking to you. Where's my drink?"

Again the bartender, trying his best, nodded his head to acknowledge the order, and went back to mixing drinks.

The Brit couldn't wait. "You bastard!" he roared.

Reaching across the bar, he grabbed the bartender by his jacket, pulled him across the bar, threw him to the floor, and punched him in the face. It took Bill, Jacob, a few of the guests, and me to pull the soldier off the poor man, and four Askaris to hold him and escort him all the way out the main gate.

Bill was furious. He yelled for all the British army men to hear, "This is a *harambee,* a time of togetherness. Either live with it or get the hell out!"

The party broke up soon after that; there was too much tension. A few of us lingered until everybody had left, and I sent Kellen down to check on the lions. Minutes later he came rushing up, out of breath and white in the face.

"Ralph—Zamba's gone!"

I wasn't sure I had heard him correctly.

"I looked everywhere! The door to the compound was open, and he's gone!" Kellen was swaying back and forth in shock.

We rushed to the lion house, and sure enough, the main door was open. The door to Zamba's room was also ajar. There were no Askaris around. Both Zamba Jr. and Tammy were pacing their rooms, nervous and upset.

I was frantic, and began the search even before the Askari captain had been called. He alerted his men, who searched the grounds. There was no moon, and with only flashlights to light our way, it was difficult to see anything. Many of the Askaris were visibly shaken, afraid to go walking out in the dark looking for a lion. I understood their fear, but it needed to be done. Even if there had been no foul play, and Zamba had simply gotten out, he was still in very serious danger if he got into the bush. There were elephants, buffaloes, and other lions in close proximity to the club, and any of these were capable of killing Zamba on sight.

The producers were frantic. If we didn't find him we would have to close down the production. He was the star: no lion, no film.

Morning broke. We hadn't slept all night. Kellen, Pippa, the Askaris, and many of the crew were still out looking and calling Zamba, to no avail.

I went back to my cottage to get a cup of coffee. As I turned the doorknob, I noticed a bit of fur stuck in the doorjamb.

"Zamba!" I yelled.

Taking the piece from the door, I ran down to the hotel and found the Askari captain.

"Are you sure it's Zamba's fur? It could be a piece of fur from a Masai spear. After a kill, they clip a piece from the lion's mane and tie it to the tip of their spear. Isn't it possible?"

He was right, I thought. It could be any lion's fur.

"Was there a note?" he asked.

"Nothing."

There was no sign of Zamba that day, or the next, or the next. My heart was sick, and I couldn't sleep, imagining what he might be going through. As the days wore on, the chances that we'd find him grew more and more remote. The studio flew an insurance man in from England, to determine whether we could continue the shoot. He said that if Zamba wasn't back in two days, and in good health, we'd have to shut down the production.

The producers were ready to pack up and leave. They realized that there was no other lion, not even Zamba Jr., who could safely work with a child, and that's what the whole movie was about. I'm sure Junior could have done it, but my promise to Pamela's mother was never far from my mind, and her faith in me weighed on my mind. Nothing was worth the risk.

I felt a grief so deep over Zamba's disappearance that I thought I would never recover. But even in my pain, I realized that everyone was being terrific. I was receiving support from everybody. Pippa was my constant companion: warm, loving, and supportive. She never lost faith that Zamba was out there, and okay, waiting to be returned to us, and her positive attitude kept me going even when my mood got very dark.

I felt sure that he'd been taken. If someone had just opened his door and let him wander out, Zamba would eventually have come to the people at the hotel instead of wandering into the forest. I shared my thoughts with the Askari captain. He agreed with my thinking and ordered a patrol to start a search of all the nearby villages, questioning locals to see if they knew anything. We knew chances were slim that people would volunteer information because of the possibility of retribution, but we thought it was worth a shot. The captain also offered a reward.

More days passed. We had called the airlines to arrange transportation for Kellen and the two lions back to the States. I couldn't eat or do anything but feel desperate and depressed about Zamba.

Suddenly a message arrived over the shortwave radio.

"We've received news of your lion. Come quickly."

The note, written on a badly stained and ripped piece of club stationery, was in English and Swahili. It was from an unknown source, but they'd provided directions—up the mountain to the bamboo village. The note said that Zamba could be found in the second village there. I was shaking from head to toe. Pippa and I hopped in a Land Rover packed with a whole bunch of Askari and headed to the specified place.

"Did the message say if he was alive?" I asked.

"No."

The captain cautioned me that it might be a hoax, and warned me not to get my hopes up. The directions took us up a rough black cotton road way back into the bamboo forest. We were slipping and sliding all the way, and getting stuck at every turn. Eventually a few of the men jumped out of the Rover and walked alongside, helping to keep it on the road, pushing when necessary.

After about an hour, we arrived at a rundown village, where the local people worked, cutting bamboo. Rows of shacks lined the muddy road that ran down the center. Half-wild, half-starved dogs roamed the town, and junk—a burned-out car, rusty and broken farm equipment—was piled up everywhere. The people stood back and watched us drive through, hidden in the doorways and shadows.

We piled out of the Rover and fanned out to search the village. Some of the Askaris tried threatening the villagers in an attempt to get some answers, but nobody would say anything. Pip and I stood in the middle of the street.

"The captain was right," I said sadly, my voice shaking. "It is a hoax."

Then I heard a familiar "AUGH!"

"Zamba?" I said, looking frantically around.

Again the "AUGH!"

"Zamba—where are you?"

Pip and I looked at the same time to a large tarp crumpled off to the side of the street, the kind that was usually used to keep maize and other supplies safe from the rain. Rushing over, we pulled and tugged until it came loose.

"Zamba! Oh my God! Hi, baby!"

Stuffed into a small, heavy, bamboo cage was my Zamba. He was thin, with bloody scrapes on his sides where he had been rubbing against the bars. His mouth and gums were also bloody; he had been trying to escape by chewing on the thick bamboo. The cage was so small that he couldn't turn around, and he had been sleeping in his own feces. There was no water or food; a stinking dead rat hung from its tail inside the cage.

We pulled apart one side of the cage until Zam could squeeze out. As soon as he was free, he fell to the ground, exhausted from malnutrition.

My fury that anyone could be so cruel took second place to my joy that Zamba was alive. I got down and gave him a hug, as dirty and smelly as he was, and he responded, despite his weakness, rolling over with me in the mud. I began to laugh and laugh as relief from the stress of waiting hit me, and he mumbled and grunted as if telling me his story. I was just so grateful that his ordeal had ended! Tears coursed down my cheeks. Zamba was back.

We never did find the people responsible for taking Zamba. The captain did not believe it had been the Mau Mau. He explained, "If it had been, Zamba would had been cut up and his skin sent back to you in a basket. No, this was someone else."

"Maybe someone has a grudge against the production company?"

"We know the two Askaris on duty at the lions' compound that night have disappeared."

"Do you think they did it?"

"It's more likely that they were paid to help. We'll probably never know. But I think that once they'd done it, for whatever reason, they couldn't handle it. Ultimately, what did they get out of it? Nothing. Something went wrong, I'm sure."

"Well, I hope they don't try again."

"If they do, we'll be ready for them."

It took a number of weeks for Zamba's sores to heal. The makeup lady had to cover his wounds for the camera. Needless to say, Zamba had a lot of company every night after that. We all took turns sleeping with him for fear something would happen again. He received a lot of paw holding and got a little tiny bit spoiled. He was worth it.

22

During the next few weeks, Zamba seemed a bit uncomfortable. He was edgy and disinterested, slow to respond to my requests, and he hadn't been sleeping or eating well. At first I thought it might be residual anxiety from his kidnapping ordeal, but when it continued for a while, I began to recognize the mood he was in, and I thought I knew what he needed.

Although Zamba was a "people person," he needed downtime the same as anyone else. We all have to get away once in a while. At the ranch, whenever he became restless, I would take him up to see our spectacular tree, the Old Lady. It wasn't so much a getaway as a return, a trip back to a place that held wonderful memories. The visit offered us a little tranquillity, away from the humdrum and stressful routine of everyday life.

When we'd return from seeing her, I'd have my old Zamba back again. His appetite would return to normal and his mood would improve; it was miraculous what a little vacation could do. But we were in Africa now, and there was no Old Lady in sight. I had a moment of anxiety, wondering if another place could recharge Zamba's batteries the way the Old Lady could. I didn't know, but there was only one way to find out.

I asked the Wildlife Authority for a special permit to take Zam into my favorite game reserve. This was obviously a very odd request: usually people went to the reserve to look at the animals that were already there, not to bring their own. I had a long conversation with Kabui, the head game warden. He was concerned about the safety issues, but he also knew Zamba, and how special he was. He and his family had their pictures taken with Zamba during production, and I could tell he wanted to help us.

"Very well. You have become like a brother Kenyan, Bwana, and so we will allow it, but only if you take two of our Askaris with you."

I had wanted to be alone with Zamba. This was his time, our time. I was always happy to answer the inevitable questions— "How did you befriend him?" "How much does he weigh?"—from strangers, but the purpose of the trip was to get him *away* from that kind of attention, and back to something more natural.

"Okay," I said, "but I want to bring my own men."

After a small huddle we agreed I could provide my own men as long as they were comparable to their Askaris. No problem there! I choose two warriors who had been assigned to the production. One was my driver, Masai, and the other was named Kapeno. Kapeno, like Masai, was a tall, lean, full-blooded moran warrior, one of the Masai. They each carried a seven-foot spear and a *rungu,* a weapon made from a single piece of wood with a massive ball at the end, the bulbous root of a certain tree. In their belts they carried knives sheathed in buffalo hide. Crisscross necklaces made of three strands of red, white, and black beads lay on their chests. They spoke their native tongue, Maasai. Masai had marked the lower half of his face and neck with ocher clay from the banks of a nearby river, which was a sign of independence and elegance. We had become good friends over time. They were proud to be chosen to accompany Zamba and me.

We left very early, around sunrise. I had packed some lunches with a few cold drinks. I'd also filled a jerry can, a rectangular metal can with a cap chained to the top, with water. All four of us drove out to the game reserve as if we were setting out for a very unconventional picnic. When we arrived at the gate, Zamba had his head sticking out of the open-air roof hatch. The guard was obviously quite taken aback by the arrangement, but he honored our permit. He checked it over and chatted with the Masai, then allowed us entry.

The reserve was stunningly beautiful; I had been there many times, and was to return many more, but it never failed to leave me breathless. The African veldt stretched for miles in all directions, its rolling vistas dotted with acacia trees. The Mara River flowed snakelike through it, following the path that the recent floods had set for it. There was not a cloud in the sky as the sun rose over the Esoit Oloololo escarpment, far to the west, and I could tell it was going to be an extremely hot day.

We drove well along the upper reaches of the Mara in search of an area where we could get out and stretch our legs. The safest places were on high hilltops, which meant we could see for miles. The grass was a bit shorter there than it was in the valleys—bad for stalkers, good for us. We were worried only about certain animals, specifically elephants, lions, buffaloes, and rhinos. Crocs and hippos could also be a bit of a threat, but we were planning to stay a good distance from the river.

As we drove deeper into the countryside, I noticed Zamba's behavior changing. The listless, tired animal we had left the club with was gone, and in his place was a sharp-eyed, active, and alert African lion.

We found a perfect spot to stop on top of a small windswept hill. I jumped Zam out of the Rover. He stretched his legs and gave a huge yawn. I gave him some water from the jerry can. The Masai filled some thermoses, and we headed out into the massive Masai Mara, one of the most splendid game reserves in Africa. I took off Zamba's leash, giving him a feeling of independence and freedom, and yet he never left my side.

So there we were: two Masai, a white man, and an African lion, walking across the veldt. I think each of us felt very lucky to be sharing such a trek. In the near distance, far enough not to pose a threat, a herd of Cape buffaloes stood motionless, looking at us. Their beautiful heads resembled the carved statues sold in the local *dukas*, or marketplaces. Small birds called oxpeckers landed on the buffaloes' backs and faces, picking dudus—small insects—from their ears, noses, eyes, and mouths. A line of giraffes moved in slow motion, turning their heads toward us, then continuing on.

Zamba's gaze was not on the animals, however. He looked to the horizon as if he were waiting for someone important, someone a long time coming. Occasionally he stopped, stood rigid as a statue for a minute, and then moved on. I encouraged him to take his time; we were there for him, after all.

I followed the Masai, knowing that they were the keepers of the land. We crossed the ridge and started down into the mouth of a valley. Kapeno went ahead to check things out, and a half hour later, we saw his small figure in the distance, waving us to come. I was a little surprised that he was waving us into a valley, but this was his country. I usually stayed on the veldt, where you could see what was coming from a long way off.

Kapeno had chosen an exceptionally beautiful place to rest; so beautiful it hardly looked real, more like heaven than a place on earth. Thick lime-green grass covered the slopes that swept down into a valley of the most beautiful jacaranda trees I have ever seen. They were in full bloom, and their vivid, bright purple blossoms covered the trees in astonishing profusion. The flowers were so thick that you couldn't see the trunks of the trees from the hillside, and the floor of the valley was lushly carpeted with blooms that had already fallen.

It was on this carpet that Zamba decided to sleep away the afternoon. As he lowered his massive body onto the sweet-scented blanket, the flowers swirled up around him. The grove of trees gave soothing protection from the sun. A slight breeze blew across a bubbly stream, cooling the air. I turned to Kapeno.

"Do you think lions appreciate beauty such as this, or is it just another valley to him?" We both thought about the question. I continued, "Do you think he appreciates the white billowing cloud, the mountain peaks, the iridescent sheen of the starling the way you and I do?"

Kepeno thought for some time. When he finally spoke, it was as if he had given the question to a higher-up and had come back with the correct answer. He was quite sure of himself.

"I do not believe so. Their beauty comes in a different form— the ability to have a successful kill, sopping up the warm innards afterward, drinking water from a cool spring after a long, hot, dry walk. These are things of beauty to a lion, not the smell of a flower."

I was taken aback by the eloquence of his answer, and thought he was probably right. But there was a little voice inside me that was sure Zamba could smell and appreciate the gorgeous flowers around him.

I chose a spot under a giant jacaranda with low-hanging

branches across from Zamba, so I could watch him sleep. I was close enough to see him, but far enough to give him the privacy he seemed to need. The Masai preferred to stay together under a tree close to mine. They assured me that the grove was safe and they would keep watch.

I had carried in my pack a small cotton hammock, which I rigged onto the tree's lower branches. Masai took a thin impala skin from his back and draped it over the hammock. I nodded my thanks, eased into the hammock, and draped the impala skin over my head to keep out the light, and any flying or crawly things wishing to join me, leaving a small opening to see through.

A slight breeze swayed the branches, gently rocking the hammock. I lay back, closed my eyes, and drifted off into one of the all-time best naps of my life.

A few hours had passed when I woke up suddenly. Something had disturbed me. I couldn't explain it, but I trusted my instinct; it was something Zamba had taught me. If there was any unusual movement or a strange noise—anything at all out of the ordinary—when I was sleeping, I would wake immediately, ready for anything. I opened my eyes.

Not a leaf stirred. Everything was quiet—too quiet? The narrow opening in the impala skin allowed me to see out, across the grove, to Zamba, still lying in a sea of flowers. At that moment, he got up on his haunches and stared at me. His look was as intent as when he stalked an animal. I didn't move.

A light breeze stirred the grove, sending the petals swirling into the air. The wind picked up a little, keeping the blossoms afloat, turning the grove into a fairyland of dancing purple blooms. They moved faster and faster, obstructing visibility like a snowstorm of blooms. I could see Zamba moving toward me through the purple haze.

He walked with his head high and his gait loose, petals in his mane. He looked absolutely stunning. His gaze never left me. What was he doing? He knew I was asleep. Whatever was on his mind wouldn't require my participation, obviously. As he got close to me, I felt more than a little confused. What was he trying to do?

I had never been scared of Zamba, not even once, but I had also never seen this kind of display. As he came closer and closer, I wondered why the Masai didn't take note. My hand was at about the same height as his head, inches from his mouth and fangs. I will admit that my whole body turned cold when he sniffed my hand, just as I had seen him do to meat before eating it. Then, putting his head in the air, he made a grimace. I could smell his body oils and his sweat, and the heavy odor of the crushed petals he'd been sleeping on. He stood still for a moment. My heart was racing in my chest.

Then, lowering his head, he put his ears back, squinted his eyes, and gently pushed his head into my hand.

In that one moment, I went from complete confusion to total ecstasy. Zamba knew! He felt the special quality of this moment, and he wanted to share it with me, the way people do when they're in a special place of beauty, joining each other in wonder. I felt very strongly that Zamba was acknowledging his love for me. It must have been a very powerful feeling, powerful enough for him to leave his comfortable bed and come to share it with me. How wonderful!

I ran my fingers across his broad head. He closed his eyes, enjoying my touch. Then, as though we did this every day, he stopped, yawned, and settled himself underneath my hammock. I, too, fell into a deep sleep, one of the most restorative ones of my life.

When we woke up again, the horizon was glowing deep red. Although evenings on the veldt were incredibly beautiful and rich with wildlife, evening was the most dangerous time of the day. We headed back to the Rover. As we went, we heard the roar of a lion in the far distance, almost too far to be audible. Zamba stopped, sniffing the air. We were on someone else's territory. I felt pressure at my side as he pressed hard against me. He raised his head, and without warning, roared back. I can count on one hand the number of times I have heard Zamba roar spontaneously—its power and the sheer noise of it, always shocked me deeply. A moment later, the lion in the distance roared again—and this time, it was clear that he was closer.

Zamba was in danger. He'd never hold his own against a lion in the wild—but it wasn't going to come to a showdown if I had anything to do with it. We walked faster, and with tremendous relief, piled into the Rover. We'd gotten what we came for—maybe even more. And so we headed home.

23

About a week after our return, we were shooting some scenes with a second-unit crew, a much smaller operation than the first unit, up on the Laikipia plateau, an hour and a half's drive from the club.

The scene called for a "battle" between two big male lions over a lioness, so all three lions were with us. Kellen and I had been rehearsing with the lions at the compound for the last week, and we felt they were ready for their shot. Masai had made sure that the lions had had a good breakfast that morning, and everything was in place; all we needed now was the sun, which was trying its best to break through the cloud cover.

The director, figuring we had another couple of hours to go before the weather cleared, asked if Kellen could go back to the club to pick up some additional lights and a small generator. He felt that with the inclement weather, more light might be needed, and we were the only ones with a big enough truck to haul the gear. Normally Kellen and I stay together when the lions are on location, because you never know when an emergency might arise. But Junior and Tammy were asleep in their portable cages, and Zamba was reclining on the special giant lounging pad the crew had made for him. A sign above the pad featured a huge star, with the word "ZAMBA" outlined in gold beneath. Talk about spoiled! Anyhow, I figured it would be safe for Kellen to go.

It wasn't but an hour after Kellen left that the weather turned bad. One of the dark, ominous clouds that had been hiding behind the ridge appeared above us, and we knew we were in for it. Within a matter of minutes, the whole sky darkened, and a deluge of rain hit—hard. Some lucky crew members crowded into the remaining trucks, but there wasn't enough room for all of us, so we quickly staked up a canvas sheet over the only soft, comfortable place there was: Zamba's pad. Then we all clambered under the tarp, huddling around Zam to keep warm and dry. We hoped it would be a short-lived rain, but as time wore on it just seemed to get worse. Needless to say, Zamba was a little put out by our invasion of his privacy.

The director decided to head back before the roads became impassable. We had been stuck a number of times before, sometimes for the better part of a day, and we didn't want it to happen again. The second unit had two Rovers and a pickup—just enough room to carry the crew and some of the paraphernalia, in other words. The rest of the equipment could be covered up with tarps and set against the rocks for shelter. One Askari, a well-trained Turkana warrior, would stay and watch the equipment. He had only his spear, but the formidable reputation of his people was well known in the area.

There was only one problem remaining: transporting the lions, when Kellen had their truck back at the club.

We were going to have to wait out the storm, at least until someone could come back for us with the truck. Zamba and I had come upon a huge cave near the shooting location on one of our many walks. The path leading to it had reminded us of the trail leading up to the Old Lady. I decided to take the lions there.

"At least it's warmer in there, and out of the rain," I explained to the assistant director.

"You can't take all three by yourself," said the A.D. "It's too dangerous."

He was right about one thing. There was no way I could have a leash on all three at the same time. But I knew that the others would follow Zamba, rather than be left alone.

"Don't worry, we'll be fine. If I leave the lions out in this weather, we risk them catching colds and getting sick. Kellen's on the way, and he'll be here soon. Just leave me one of the walkie-talkies. I'll keep in touch."

I threw on a rain parka, tucking the walkie-talkie in an inside pocket, and grabbed a flashlight, a pack of matches, some prewrapped sandwiches, and three cat chains. I threw two of them over my shoulder, and fastened the third around Zamba's neck.

I swung open the doors to Junior and Tammy's cages, yelling over the sound of the rain, "Come on, guys, let's go. Up and at 'em."

And then I motioned to Zam. All adult male lions hate rain. Their manes get so heavy with water, they can barely hold their heads up. I could tell that Zamba really didn't want to leave his executive quarters, but as the crew had already crowded all their equipment into his lair, leaving little room for him, he gave up, moaned his displeasure, and walked out into the wetness.

Tammy looked to Zamba as her mate, despite his constant disinterest, which was a heartbreak for me. I had tried, on a number of occasions, to set these two up, and Tammy was certainly up for it, but Zamba never reciprocated her feelings, rebuffing her most ardent advances. I would have loved for him to find a lady friend, but it wasn't to be. But Tammy's unrequited love served me well that night, since she'd follow him anywhere. So when she saw he was going, she bounced out into the rain after him. Junior hesitated at first, then with a low growl, took up the rear.

Thank goodness Zamba and I had been to the cave before. He knew where we were going, and moved along quite well.

"Junior! Move it. Tammy, come on, girl," I called back over my shoulder. Heads down, bodies soaking wet, they moved out into the storm.

"We'll tell Kellen to look for you in the cave!" shouted the director after us.

"Okay," I yelled. Kellen had never been there before, but I figured I would be able to guide him using the walkie-talkie when he arrived.

"Good luck!" yelled one of the crew.

"Be careful!" yelled another.

The wind was picking up, and the sky was a mass of turbulent thunderheads. Junior would stop every so often to take refuge under a big tree, but when he saw we weren't stopping, he'd slap his tail in anger and follow so he wouldn't lose us in the darkening forest. What seemed like a nice short walk when the weather was good was now a strenuous climb, filled with obstacles. The mud was treacherously slippery, falling branches and huge granite boulders blocked our way at every turn. The rain was coming down in sheets, hitting us with a force that made it difficult for the lions to stay on their feet.

We walked a good distance into the forest, then up a rocky incline to reach the cave. Its entrance, located on the side of a mountain, was partly blocked by an enormous fallen tree. I started to dig down under the tree to allow us to enter.

"Come on, Zam. You know how. A little help, please."

He knew the command for dig, and dig he did—not necessarily in the right place, but it was of some help. When the hole was big enough, Zamba crouched down and squeezed under the log, and I scrambled in behind him. We managed to clear the entrance and crawled up into the cave.

A high pitched "augh" from outside reminded me I still had two lions out there in the rain, getting ever more soaked by the minute. They were standing on the other side of the tree, drenched to the bone, looking like two giant, drowned rats. I could see they needed a little direction. Going back out, I pushed and shoved them into the right position to get under the tree and into the entrance. No go. They stood there looking into the dark bowl of the cave, and it was clear that there was no way they were going to launch themselves into the unknown.

"You guys are lions, remember? Nothing frightens a lion. Right?"

I pushed by them and scrambled into the cave, illuminating the walls with my flashlight so they could see there was no bogeyman inside.

"Come on, you guys, it's warm. Tammy girl, let's go."

Once she saw me and Zamba inside, she was up and on her way without any hesitation. Junior followed.

Although the opening was small, the cave went back a lot farther than I'd remembered. In some places, the ceiling was a good ten or fifteen feet high. I put my gear against the wall and gathered some wood for a fire. There were a number of pieces of old dried bark, twigs, and branches lying about, and a whole small dead tree. I could tell that both animals and people had used this cave many times in the past. I collected some dried animal feces to help start the fire.

"I hope nobody else chooses to use the cave tonight. They'll be in for quite a surprise."

It only took a few matches to get the kindling to light. Within minutes, we had a blazing fire. Junior was the first to shake himself, spraying water everywhere, and the others followed suit. Zamba nearly put out the fire. Then, quite content with himself, he settled in, lying at my side. Tammy sniffed and smelled the damp moss growing on the rocks. She licked the wetness, and grimaced at the taste.

A swarm of bats swooped down to check us out. Junior had never seen anything like these silent "birds." Alarmed, he snarled and leaped away, stumbling over the dead tree before he could get his footing. Tammy thought he'd seen something out there that she hadn't, and fell over Zamba trying to get away from it!

Zamba, God bless him, never got up. He raised his lip in a small snarl and went back to sleep. The last few bats flew around looking for places to sleep the storm away. They settled high overhead in the deep rock crevices, hanging in their upside-down world.

The warmth from the fire was beginning to take effect. My "pride" was accustomed to fire, as they had seen it many times, but I'm not sure they had understood the warmth it could bring. As it blazed, it threw strange outlines of the rock formations and the lions against the walls of the cave. The shadows dancing against the walls of the cave made the lions uneasy, and they got up, pacing back and forth watching, their eyes opened wide in wonder, snarling at each shadow, following the images as they frolicked from one rock to another. The more they moved, the more the shadows danced. The cats roamed the cave, unaware that the disturbances were of their own making.

I watched, fascinated. In my mind I saw an ancient and mythical dance, the dance of the demon lions, who came out only when darkness fell. They came out of every crack in the rock, behind every crag. It was like watching a masquerade ball, a choreographed dance in some underworld palace. The shadows were grotesque on the walls, ten times bigger than real lions, leaping from one crevice to another cranny; huddling in recesses, only to jump to a far-reaching rock across the cave, walking on the ceiling like devil acrobats.

The lion demons slowly hypnotized the big cats, and as they relaxed, their eyelids fell and their bodies succumbed to a peaceful sleep. The demons settled into the rocks, hidden until an occasional spark from the fire made one of the cats jump. My real lions lay on top of one another, blending into one another in the firelight like a sea of warm, liquid honey.

I listened to the crackling of the fire and the low rumble of the storm passing overhead. Occasionally a bolt of lightning lit up the entrance to the cave. I sat quietly, watching the lions. Junior was the farthest away, near the entrance. Although he looked up to Zamba as the head of the group, I think sometimes he felt himself the guardian and protector of the pride, maybe because Zam spent so much time with me.

I had never shared sleeping quarters with any lions other than Zamba, and I had a moment's worry—if they were going to revert back to their natural instincts, this would be a particularly poor time to do it. The feeling passed quickly; Junior and Tammy were very dear to me, and I felt embarrassed that I had allowed my mind to go there.

The scent of wet lion filled the cavern. It was a wonderful, wild aroma, the smell of the earth's true inhabitants. As I dried off and began to relax, I felt warm and cozy as I lay watching them, and the wonder of the kind of kinship I shared with them washed over me. These were carnivores; animals that ate mammals. Mammals like me. And yet we had managed to find a common ground.

I had spent my life searching for a key that would help me to communicate with wildlife, and I had chosen the lion to help me find the way. That night I truly felt that they had helped me to move a step closer to that dream. For trust surely was a form of communication, and there was no greater proof that they trusted me than their ability to sleep in my presence—and mine, to sleep in theirs.

I awoke in the morning to the sight of my "pride" piled on top of one another. They looked to the walls as they woke up, wondering where their demon friends had gone. Then, content that all was well, they all went outside to do their business. Zamba gave me a "puff" and a wide yawn. I smiled back and joined him outside to relieve myself. We gave each other side glances, as men do at the urinals.

Zamba stayed outside to groom. The rain had washed him squeaky clean, and I had never seen him looking so elegant. His mane was fluffy, and the slightest breeze blew it against his face. Each lion found a comfortable spot—Junior on top of the cave, Tammy in front, and Zamba on a broad rock just near the cave's entrance, and in a minute, they were all asleep again.

I don't think there's anything quite as beautiful as Africa the day after a storm. It seemed as if the rain had washed every microscopic bit of dirt out of the atmosphere. The slag that had covered the landscape was gone. It was a time of rebirth—everything dirty, decayed, used, soiled, or damaged had been washed away, and a new, perfect world emerged. The sky had never been bluer, or the clouds whiter, and the leaves of the trees looked as if they'd been hand-washed. Little rivulets of clear cool water coursed their way down the hills into the valley below, finding their mother river and joining her to swell her banks and moisten the dry land far below. This must have been how Creation looked on the first day.

The walkie talkie beeped. "Ralph, old boy, you there?"

24

The big day had finally come—the day I was to "fight" Zamba in the film. I awoke early, showered, shaved, put on my khaki shorts and Western shirt, threw a sweater over my shoulders, and headed down to the compound. Pip was already there, with Njoka and Masai. I gave Zamba his good morning hug and we went to work, giving him a thorough grooming, combing out any early morning mats in his mane. Masai and Pip picked out any dodo bugs that had set up house in his fur. We were all a bit silent, anticipating the task ahead of us, and even Zamba seemed to feel the tension in the air.

We rode down to the set in the Rover. To get there, we had to drive through a rough, desolate area called Rumaruti. Deep crevices, rocks, and raging streams all helped to make the ride an uncomfortable, bumpy trip. Zamba eased himself up through the sunroof opening and rested his front paws on the roof of the car. With his huge head, massive chest, and mane sticking well above the opening, he rode like a monarch touring his kingdom. Making slow progress, we passed a small group of Masai walking tall, all decked out in their brightly colored garments, skin dyed ocher, and each carrying a spear. I waved. They waved back, and then froze at the sight of Zamba, who let out his usual guttural growl in greeting.

At last, we arrived at the set. As I pulled through the gate, Langjo, the security guard, saluted me. He was barefoot and dressed in khaki shorts and a brown short-sleeved shirt with epaulets, carrying a spear.

"*Jambo,* Bwana Simba!" he said, with a broad grin.

"*Jambo,* Langjo." I smiled back. After checking with the assistant director, I unloaded Zamba and put him in a specially built enclosure. The sun had come out, and the grass and shrubs were drying off. Feeling great, Zamba took off, leaping around in his new enclosure, occasionally slipping on the morning dew and falling on his face. In this cold, crisp morning air he would certainly give a great performance on film.

There was a lot of quiet excitement on the set. Although everyone was looking forward to the fight, everyone was aware of the danger involved. It was unusual for someone to wrestle an animal of Zamba's size. Many trainers would wrestle "young adult" lions, but people didn't generally take on a big five-hundred-pounder. There were a number of reasons for this. The obvious one, of course, is that a big animal is harder to control than a smaller one. We also had to make sure that we didn't accidentally wrestle too long and confuse the cat by stimulating a sexual response. It's also easier to wrestle with a younger lion because the young adults still have a cub's playing instincts. A mature lion no longer "plays" as he did when he was a cub. Instead, he has to be taught to simulate an attack, to pretend to do exactly what he would do if he was making a kill, without really biting or exposing his claws. This is hard with an adult: sometimes, like human actors, they could get caught up in the moment. Their natural instincts would take over and a mouth hold would become a real bite.

Zamba would have to fight me, controlled only by our affection for each other. When he raced at me and launched himself into full attack mode, only his years of training would tell him to pull his punches. When his massive paw slapped me across the face, or when my arm was between his fangs, the quiet words I was speaking into his ear would guide him, and my hand on his mane would direct him.

There was another factor adding to our nerves. The crew was buzzing with news of a young woman in a neighboring town, supposedly an animal expert, who had accidentally been killed by her own lion, a three-year-old male about the size of Junior. She had tied him out and left him for a little while, and when she came back he had greeted her by jumping up on her, the way he always did. But when she told him to get down, he had slid his front feet down her shoulders instead of jumping down, and one of his dewclaws had hooked the carotid artery in her neck. She bled to death in about a minute or so. They said the lion never realized what he had done, and continued to play with her while she was on the ground dead.

It was a sad story, and I had heard many stories like it over the course of my career. When you are dealing with such a powerful animal, you have to teach each other how to act. They have to learn how strong they are, and to handle us with care. Even so, accidents will happen. It's just a risk you have to take when you work with an exotic.

It was time for makeup, but this was to be no ordinary makeup session. I had to double as a Masai warrior, and the scene was to be shot in the rain, where regular makeup would wash off. The solution they came up with was to give me a bath in a solution called gentian violet, a long-lasting dye that would color me totally black.

Three women stripped me down and submerged me in a bathtub of the dye. When I emerged I was definitely black—all over! My skin was the color of mahogany. It was not unattractive—a good thing, since the color did not fully wash off for almost six months. Next came the Masai hairpiece, then the brilliant red wrap of cloth, and finally the spear and the knife. I stood in front of the mirror and admired the effect. My bright blue eyes were the only giveaway. Otherwise, I was a full Masai warrior, one born and raised in Chicago!

The crew had fenced in the area where the fight was to take place. They had chosen a beautiful spot high on the top of a mountain, surrounded by copper-colored rock that looked down on a lush green valley speckled with acacia trees.

As I was waiting for the final equipment to be moved away and out of the background of the shot, I reread the script. This scene was the climax of the film. The movie told the story of a Masai warrior who falls in love with a young white girl who has a full-grown lion named King for a pet. The lion's love for the girl is so strong that the warrior and the lion are forced to battle over the girl's love. In the heat of the battle, the girl's father arrives. He must decide whom to shoot: the lion, whom the girl loves, or the warrior, whom she does not. Ultimately the father shoots the lion to save the warrior's life, but the warrior dies anyway from his wounds.

The director's voice shattered my thoughts. "Attention, everybody! What we are about to do is extremely dangerous—not for us, but for Ralph. I must ask for absolute quiet."

Because 80 percent of the people in the compound were African, his words were repeated in Swahili.

A hush fell on the set. I stationed my people around the area to assist whenever necessary. The insurance company had forced the production company to have armed guards on the set whenever the lions were working. I was livid when I found out, and threatened to pull out. I told them that I would never allow a person with a gun on the set. Many of the stunts we did looked dangerous, and weren't—what if they made a mistake and shot? I couldn't risk leaving such a decision up to an untrained person. Even if they were stopping something that had gotten out of control, anything less than a perfect shot could enrage the animal even more, increasing the danger.

They finally agreed to arm the guards with tranquilizer guns. This was even stupider; by time the drug worked, the lion would have ample time to finish whatever mayhem he'd begun. But it appeased them, so I let it be, with strict instructions that no one was to shoot unless Kellen or I gave the order.

I picked up my props, a spear and knife, and entered the fenced-in area. From the moment I walked in, it seemed that time stood still, that my movements were in slow motion.

Kellen had placed Zamba in the enclosure so he could get accustomed to the terrain. Zamba had climbed to a high point on one of the cliffs, and was looking over the valley below. With his head held high, and his mane whipped by the mountain breeze, he sniffed at the Africa of his ancestors, and at that moment, I was very conscious that he had traded their survival-of-the-fittest ethos for my friendship. I felt uneasy, as if I was invading his personal thoughts, the territory of his mind.

I needed to talk with Zamba before we started shooting. More importantly, I needed him to smell me, so that he'd know that this black man was me. His back was to me as he stood looking out over the veldt, and I approached him cautiously. When I was a few yards from him, I called his name, breaking his concentration.

"Hey, Zam, you ready for the big fight?"

Zamba put his ears back, and for the second time ever, he snarled at me. It wasn't just a lifted lip or a complaint, but a real, live, lion snarl. He got up on his haunches and looked at me, and I realized how he must seem to other people. His eyes were red, small, and piercing, and there was no recognition in them. I felt a chill run down my back.

"Zamba, baby, it's me."

I started to walk toward him. He was still snarling, and his ears were flashing back and forth, radioing his confusion. I could tell he was thinking, *It's him . . . it's not him.* I was stunned by the effect my color change had on him. The dye was certainly convincing: I was pretty sure that regular makeup wouldn't have had this drastic an effect. It wasn't until I got within a few feet of him and let him smell my very nervous hand that I saw him relax. After a lot of baby talk, he finally made a conciliatory noise and pushed his head into my side.

I yelled, "Okay, we're ready!" and added, "I guess," under my breath. I still didn't feel totally comfortable.

My instructions were simple. On cue, Zamba was to race at me, leap up on his hind legs, knock me down, and wrestle. It was to look like a fight to the death.

"Okay, quiet on the set!" shouted the A.D.

"Start the rain!"

"Roll camera, and . . . action!"

The cameras were rolling. I gave Zamba the cue to attack. He turned and looked at me. My God, that look! At that moment, with his ears back, body low to the ground, and every muscle tensed, he wasn't the gentle lion I knew. Then he came at me. From outside the enclosure, Pam was screaming her lines, "No, Father! Don't shoot! Please, Father, don't kill him! Don't kill King!!"

For a nanosecond I saw something unrecognizable in Zamba's eyes. What was I seeing? What was he seeing? Was he still seeing an unfamiliar African tribesman, instead of his beloved Ralph?

He had never come at me so strongly, with such determination. Years of training allowed me to stay loose and agile, ready for the hit—I knew that if any part of me tensed up and resisted, I'd break in two. And then he sprang, five hundred pounds of feline power. Six times stronger than a man, he hit me like a ton of swinging bricks. His great front legs and paws gathered me up like a toy and carried me through the air, his mane choking my breath. Then I hit the ground, and did a tuck and roll with Zamba right after me. For a split second, I was allowed to roll out from under him, but he attacked again and again, until his great weight held me to the ground. His eyes narrowed, and his mouth opened to display four inches of fang.

I threw out my arm to protect my face, and as I did so, I flashed to another time, another place, when another lion had me in the same position and sank his fang into my arm. I could see the scar, glistening under the black dye.

Zamba's fangs locked around my wrist and held—softly. Yes, softly. Even with the dye that had rendered me unrecognizable, the girl screaming and the man yelling in the background, and the excitement of the moment, our affection for each other was enough. Our great love for each other was stronger than tradition, stronger than instinct itself.

Then the father shot the rifle, and Zamba was "fatally wounded." I broke the squibs that we had placed earlier under his mane, and the "blood" ran down his chest. Screaming and crying, "King! King!" Pam hugged and caressed Zamba. His great head fell into her lap as he "died."

The cameras stopped rolling. There was a moment of silence,

and then pandemonium broke out. Amid applause, laughter, and cries of "Bravo," I got up and walked over to Zamba. As I looked down at his still and bloody form, sheer terror shot through me at the horrible thought of his really being taken from me. I bent down over him. One great amber eye opened, and a forepaw shot up and caught me around the neck. He pulled me to him, and with his big, raspy tongue, he licked my face.

We got up and walked out of the compound, out of my world of fakery and applause, and into the wilderness of his.

25

The heaviest rains usually come between March and June, but this was a year of floods, and the heavy rains had come early, so we had been given a few days off while we waited for the weather to clear. My Turkana friend Shilingi and I had decided to go off on our own for a couple of days, and I decided to take Zamba along for the ride. He loved driving with his head sticking out the top of the Land Rover.

Shilingi was an interesting character. He was a brilliant tracker and a strident conservationist. I found out many years later that it was the zealotry of the converted—he had been a poacher in his youth. His tracking skills and eye for detail made him an incredible person to safari with; he saw all kinds of things on the trail that a normal person would never even notice, and I always felt very safe with him. He carried a small bag of snuff, and he would often stop, take a pinch, and gaze off into the distance. Suddenly, some wonderful animal would then appear. We used to joke that the snuff made them come. "Take some snuff, Shilingi," we'd bug him, if there was nothing doing on the veldt.

We were on our way to Satuk through the Laikipia outback to see my good friend Simon Evans, who owns and operates a camel safari. This region is usually quite dry, but when it does rain, there are stretches of black cotton roads that are impossible to travel. The recent storm had lasted for the better part of a week, and some of those roads were not much better than swamps. In some cases they had disappeared completely.

Fishtailing our four-wheel drive Rover around a corner, we found ourselves confronted with a body of water that stretched in all directions for a good three hundred feet. We were already committed, so we gave it all we had, in the hopes that the momentum would carry us through the mud. It didn't. Halfway through we sank right into it, the wheels spinning us deeper and deeper. We saw signs of the road rising out of the swamp about a hundred feet ahead on the other side.

We waded through the muck to see what we were up against. The road ahead had a base of gravel and had held up quite well. It was just the spot where the Rover was bogged down that had filled with water. It looked like a torrent of water had come down the gully going quite fast and hit the road, washing it away and leaving only mud in its place.

We spent a few hours jacking up the Rover, putting brush under the wheels, lowering the jack, and slowly creeping ahead a few feet—over and over and over. It was slow, hard work. I took Zamba out of the Rover and tied him to a nearby log so he wouldn't wander while we were working.

The three of us were taking a break under an acacia tree when out of the bush came four warriors. They were all wearing the customary red *shuka*s, full-length, dresslike tunics, and red, black, and white beads crossed their chests; and each carried a spear and a machete held by a skin belt. All wore shoes cut from a car tire. One huge man walked directly up to us. Zamba stood up and emitted a low growl. The man ignored the potential threat and gave us a broad grin.

"*Sopa,*" he said, using the Masai greeting. "I know of you. You are Bwana Simba."

"Well, of this lion, at least." I smiled, surprised that we would be known this far out in the bush. I calmed Zamba with a command to lie down.

The man spoke a fair bit of English, and we exchanged some small talk about Zamba. To my embarrassment, he was very impressed by my ability to control Zamba. The more I tried to explain to him that it was a matter of training behaviors, the more he insisted that I had some godlike power.

In the meantime, the other warriors had been looking—and laughing—at the situation with the Rover. A few got to pushing it, causing it to rock back and forth.

"Well, we have come to help," said the big man.

"How did you know we were here?"

The big fellow laughed.

"Jungle drums," he said, then laughed aloud again.

He knew what to do with the Rover. He said something in an African dialect I didn't understand, but which Shilingi recognized as Dorobo. Almost in unison, the warriors thrust the butts of their spears into the ground and took out their machetes, walking off into the bush. We heard a good deal of Dorobo being spoken, along with the hacking of brush, and then moments later they reappeared dragging huge, dead trees behind them. For the next two hours, we helped them build a road of brush through the muck to the gravel road. Then, with Zamba in the back to give the

Rover some weight, everybody started pushing. With the engine roaring, the Rover slipped and slid the hundred feet to the gravel road. A cheer went up as the tires cleared the muck and hit hard dirt again. Everybody was covered in mud and smiling.

The biggest smile was on the big headman, who slapped his muddy hand in mine.

"We are so happy you got stuck," he said. I was shocked at his words and could only look at him, puzzled. "If you had not gotten stuck, we would not have been able to help you."

Then, with a wave, the warriors pulled their spears from the ground and disappeared into the bush.

26

The rain had held up production for months, and when it finally stopped, we worked day and night to take advantage of the weather. After a couple of months of this grueling pace, it became clear to the producers that everyone on the set was exhausted, pure and simple.

So they gave the performers and crew a couple of weeks off to go on safari and see a bit of the country before finishing the rest of the filming. Pip and I were looking for an out-of-the-way place—something different and exciting, and yet relaxing. We were still discussing where to go as we drove into Nanyuki one afternoon to buy some supplies for the house.

We stopped along the side of the road for some of the roast corn that the locals cook on small charcoal stoves, or *jikos*. These stands were quite common all over Kenya, and they fed a lot of people who hurried back and forth to work.

"Zamba had one of his moments last night," I said as we got out of the car.

"You mean seeing things that aren't there?" asked Pip, with just the slightest hint of sarcasm in her voice.

"Pip! Why do you do that?"

"Do what?" She smiled, and then: "I'm sorry. I'm just teasing."

Some extraordinary things were starting to happen as Zamba matured. He was about eight years old, and there were times when he would awaken in the middle of the night, fully alert, as if he'd heard something I hadn't, or had a bad dream. Sometimes he would sit up in bed and watch as though something was moving across the room. His moods during these episodes were unpredictable: sometimes he was gentle and warm, other times his lips formed a snarl as he watched, his eyes crimson.

These moments had gotten more frequent and more intense during the time we'd been in Africa. Once, while walking in the forest near the club, he stopped in the middle of the trail and sat down. I could see his eyes following something moving in front of him, and heard him "chuff" at it with the friendly noise lions make when they're greeting someone. The only problem: there wasn't anyone there. Pippa had seen it, too, but she was reluctant to believe there was anything unusual about it.

I thought Zamba was psychic.

In the same way that I believe that real communication between animal species—humans included—is possible—I believe that it's possible to communicate with things you can't actually see. I think some people and some animals are better at this than others, and I thought Zamba was especially gifted. Why wouldn't he be? He was a phenomenal communicator in general.

Pippa and I were arguing the point when an old woman at the corn stand interrupted us. She had clearly understood our conversation, but preferred to speak in Swahili. Although I had picked up a little of the language, I was happy that Pippa was along to interpret.

"You need to speak with a Mganga," the woman declared. She was an old Kikuyu mama, sitting on a small tree stump by the roadway and selling her corn. A ragged old skin hat was pushed down on her head, over her weather-beaten face, which showed her age to be somewhere in the eighties, maybe more. We went over to where she was sitting.

"To reach a place where your friend and you can truly communicate, you must go through a Mganga, a spiritual person. He will hold yours and God's hand, so that you may talk."

The old woman didn't seem to know we were speaking about a lion. She never looked at us. She just spoke as though anyone who cared to could listen.

"I've heard of these people," spoke Pippa. "They're called Mganga if they heal and do good, and Mchawi, which means witch doctor, if they do harm and practice *juju,* or black magic. Most are just fakers. It's rare to find an authentic one."

"To find the one you speak of, you must travel far. They are different in the North." She was looking toward us now, and I could see one of her eyes was closed, and the other had a white spot over it. She was quite blind and talking to where our voices were coming from. "He will not talk to you though," she said, and laughed.

"*Kwa nini?*" asked Pippa.

"Because you are *muzungu.*"

Because we were white.

Then, she added, "Look to the NFD. Maybe there. Or maybe no."

Then as she turned away, her hand appeared from under her *kikoi,* palm up. I paid for the roast corn, added ten shillings for the advice, and we headed for the Rover. The corn was delicious.

"What is the NFD?" I asked Pippa.

"It's the Northern Frontier District, the farthest northern region of Kenya. Dry and hot, hot, hot!"

"What do you think?"

"Think about what?"

"You know. That Magogo, whatever."

"It's Mganga. They are supposed to be in tune with the spirits of nature. I know that there are tribes who believe in them very strongly, loving and caring for them as though they are gods. There is one in particular who is supposed to be very powerful."

"Do you think the one you're thinking of and the one the old woman talks about is the same?"

"Maybe. I don't even know if I could find him." She hesitated. "If it is the same one, he wanders far into the interior of the NFD and is in great demand. The local people call him whenever they are concerned about whether or not something will happen. He's also supposed to have the ability to heal."

"Sounds like he's our man, all right," I said.

Pip had a serious expression on her face. "What's really rare is all the different tribes use him. And he moves around a great deal, so we'll probably have trouble finding him."

"Why?"

"It's a huge area, only the tribes know it well. He never stays in one place very long, and it's a very, very hot country."

"So?" I said slowly.

"So, what?" she returned, waiting.

"Well . . ." I hesitated. "Next Friday does start our time off for the holidays." I leaned back in the seat. "Zam, what do you think? Do you want a witch doctor getting into your mind?"

"Mganga," Pip corrected.

Zamba looked like he needed to pee, so that ended the conversation right there. I knew Pip loved an adventure as much as I did, and that I wouldn't have to wait long for a response.

•   •   •

A week later we were bathing Zam and loading him in the Rover. The supplies went up top on the roof canopy, behind where Zamba's hatch opened up. I threw a canvas over the whole lot, tying it down good and tight. One of my friends felt it was just too dangerous an area to go without some sort of protection, so he loaned me a 306 rifle, which I secured under the front seat. We strapped a few extra jerry cans of petrol and water to the bumper of the car, checked the tires to be sure they were well inflated, and headed out into the bush country in search of this spiritual man.

We had told only a few trusted friends where we were going. This was an intensely personal quest, one that I felt driven to complete. I knew that most people would probably think I was crazy.

The next day found us driving deep into Kenya. There were no roads to speak of, just an occasional piece of lumber, some rusty wire, empty cans, and quite a number of beer bottles. Some old miners in search of gems had probably used the track we were on. The area was noted for its precious stones, but many prospectors had died trying to find them. Animal tracks crisscrossed the old road at every turn. The animals were there, but they were not as abundant as in the areas farther south. Zamba perked up whenever some appeared, but he never showed any aggression toward them.

Few *mzungu* ever went into this area, as the tribes were noted to be quite hostile. I figured that between the gun, Pippa's fluent Swahili, and the African lion in the back, it kind of evened the odds.

The NFD lived up to its reputation. It was HOT! Our outside thermometer read 115 degrees, and we were told it had been known to reach 130 degrees at times. I checked back often to see how Zamba was taking it. This was not the best place for a lion, especially one with a full mane, but he seemed quite content to sit up high with his head and shoulders sticking out of the hatch in the roof. The dry wind whipped his mane back off his face, giving him an almost human look. I also noticed that it was tangling his mane and would make it impossible to comb, so we stopped under the only acacia tree for miles, which provided a small amount of shade. Pip got me one of her wraps, a bright orange one, and together we made a sort of enormous bandana out of it. I put as much of Zamba's mane in it as I could, then wrapped it all up like a giant ponytail and tied it tight. He looked like a washerwoman, but I didn't think he minded.

By the second day driving in the NFD, the temperature had hit 118 degrees. Zamba was beginning to breathe heavily. All the windows were already open, so we let down the back door, and even rode with ours held open to get some of the hot air circulating.

I was very worried about him getting heat stroke, and eventually we had to stop again. We poured our precious water over the kanga cloth that was draped over his head. He didn't object, but it only covered the back of his head and mane. With a nod from Pippa, I cut two large holes in another khanga, and then draped that one over his whole head and face, letting his ears stick out the holes. Then I tied it underneath his chin like a bib, and cut two more big holes so he could see out. Over this we poured some more cool water. As it ran down his nose, he caught some of it with his tongue and slurped it up—and then a gallon of our reserve water as well. He looked hysterical in his "babushka" getup, but I had to keep him as cool as possible.

The sun was beating down on him through the sunroof, so we closed it, thinking we'd reopen it later, when the sun shifted positions. The glass windows were reflecting a lot of heat into the Rover, so with a piece of the canvas that was holding down our belongings on the roof, we covered the windows. The dark interior was cooler for Zamba, although he wasn't happy about not being able to sit up and look out the top. Leaving the front doors and the back open allowed what little breeze there was to blow into the back.

We drove for hours. Suddenly we saw a cloud of billowing dust about a quarter mile in front of the Rover. As we drew closer we saw that it was caused by a gathering of perhaps forty or fifty tribesmen and a huge number of camels. They were surrounding what looked like a small well.

Fifteen or more of the men were in the throes of battle, complete with drawn sabers and spears poised to strike! Some were on camels; others were fighting on the ground. Many of the men had blood on their garments, and the camels were dripping blood as well, from slashes on their sides and legs. All the men were yelling and waving their weapons at one another.

"We had better get out of here," Pippa said, trying to remain calm.

I didn't argue, but there was no easy way out. My instinct was to slam the Rover in reverse, because some of the fighters had already seen our Rover and were running in our direction, sabers out. But the road—if you could even call it that—was so horribly rutted that we'd never be able to outdistance them.

As I was trying to figure a way around the battle, I noticed the statuesque figure of a bearded man wearing a pure white Muslim robe, astride a white camel on a small rise, away from the fighting. His camel wore red tufts on its reins and a circle of bells on its feet, and the bells could be heard whenever he moved. Three or four camels carrying women were behind him. The moment he saw us, he raised his arm, which ended the fighting.

I reached down and undid the rope holding the gun, which I passed to Pippa, telling her to hide it along my side of the seat, where I could get to it quickly if I needed it. The warriors raced down to the car and gathered around it, yelling, screaming, pushing the Rover so that it rocked back and forth.

The man on the white camel joined the throng. He was a large man with piercing dark eyes and a black beard edged in gray. His robe was of white silk, and a large golden medallion was suspended on a thick gold chain from around his neck. I could see that his saber was hanging from his waist, and that its sheath was of a cured goatskin etched in silver.

The man dismounted, stood in front of the Rover, and yelled something at us that I am sure was obscene. I remember thinking that his voice sounded exactly like the noise a Cape buffalo makes during mating season. As he approached my side of the car, he slid his saber out of its sheath and pointed it at us. I rolled down the window just enough to smell his foul breath, and felt for the trigger on the rifle under the cloth.

To my enormous surprise, he spoke English. He said, "I am Sheik Rashid Mohammed Ackubar, ruler of the northeastern province of this treacherous land, and the owner of this well. You are trespassers."

"We were only passing through," I said.

"Out! *Out!*" he commanded, attempting to open the locked door.

I had to think fast. If we got out, we'd reveal the gun, and I felt that would be a mistake.

"We can't," I said.

"You *what?*"

"If we do, it will endanger you and your people."

"What do you say? Get out, or it is you who will be endangered."

From the backseat, Zamba let out an "arghh." I reached back and took off the wraps he was wearing. He shook his head, and his mane fell down around his shoulders, the way a woman's hair will when she removes her hairpins. I turned on the overhead lights, and there was Zamba. The lights threw a halo effect onto his head and mane, and at that moment, he looked holy and not entirely of this earth.

Rashid drew back in awe when he saw him, as did the warriors who stood nearby.

"Holy Allah! What is this? What have you done to possess a lion to be under your power?"

"This is why we are here. Now you see why it could be dangerous for us to step out of the car."

"What is your name?" Rashid asked.

"Bwana Simba," I said without hesitation.

"What kind of a name is that?" he ordered.

"It is my given name."

"Only Mugu has the power to be a leader of lions."

"Mugu?"

"God," whispered Pippa.

"You shut up," said Rashid, pointing the saber at Pippa.

It was apparent that women were not allowed to speak to men—or at least this man.

"We're looking for the Manga," I said.

"Mganga," said Pippa, pinching my arm. "Mganga."

Pippa began talking directly to Rashid in Swahili, trying to explain our purpose there.

"I tell you to shut up!" he said, waving his saber. "It is not allowed!" he roared. Pippa crouched farther down in the seat. Then he turned back to me.

Staying as calm as I could, I murmured, "Well, yes, we, ah, were wondering if you could help us? We need to meet your, uh . . . Mganga."

Not taking his eyes off Zamba, he said, "He will not see you."

"Why?"

"You are white."

"That's what the old lady said," I whispered to Pippa.

I saw the sheik getting a bit disturbed and thought it would be wise to change the subject.

"Why are those men fighting?" I asked.

"They fight to let their camels drink the water. But there is only so much, and I own the well. They want to own the water. Only Mugu can own the water, but the fools claim the water is theirs. This stupid drought has lasted far too long. We are digging more wells but it takes time."

"Where we came from the land is bursting with water. Floods everywhere," I said.

"It is the way in East Africa. For centuries the NFD suffers and the south is drowning. But you have your droughts, too. It is the way of Allah."

"What will happen here?" I said.

"Some will die so the animals may live."

"That doesn't make sense, does it?"

"The camel gives us food, clothing, milk, transportation. In some cases they are worth more than their owners."

"Shouldn't you try to stop them?"

"No. It is better to let them kill each other. Then there will be less fighting."

I don't understand that kind of thinking.

Rashid, deep in thought, lowered his saber and slowly put it back in its sheath. He watched Zamba sitting quietly in the back, eyes on me. I felt the gun would not be necessary now. Finally he beckoned to one of the men standing by the camels. He looked like Lawrence of Arabia.

"This man's name is Abdulrahmin Mouhamoudin," he said. "He doesn't speak very much English, but enough. He will take you where the Mganga is. Whether he will see you or not is a question that has no answer."

Rashid motioned to have his camel brought up to him. Once mounted, he turned toward us. "I will leave you now. May Allah be with you on your quest."

And with this he, his harem, and twenty or more men mounted their camels and followed.

"Thank you," I yelled.

A wave of his hand was his acknowledgment. Pippa, Zamba, the guide, and I watched as they disappeared over the horizon.

I turned toward the man who was to take us to see the Mganga.

"Your name is . . . ? I asked.

"Abdulrahmin Mouhamoudin."

"Abdul . . . what?" I asked, as politely as I could.

He replied, "Abdulrahmin Mouhamoudin."

"Do you have something shorter? We *mzungu*—well." I gestured like a simpleton.

The man looked at us in disgust. "Choose any name and I will answer to it."

Pippa and I looked at each other and simultaneously said, "Lawrence."

"Agreed," he said.

"How long will it take?" I asked.

He shrugged his shoulders.

"How far?"

Again a shrug. "You'll see."

He didn't want to sit with Zamba, so he jumped up on the roof of the car with the luggage, wrapped his headscarf around his face, took his *shuka,* and covered himself completely.

"Which way?" I yelled up.

A long, bony finger appeared through the cloth and pointed. Putting the Rover in four-wheel drive, we followed the pointed finger.

The country we drove through was a vast desert of sand and rock, with the occasional tuft of grass. The NFD was indeed smoldering hot. I had never felt such heat.

Our course was taking us parallel with a high ridge of mountains, as barren as the desert they looked down upon. We passed a few dried-up, deserted camel wells. Scattered debris lay all around, left over from what was once a small encampment. Doom palms that had received their nourishment from the once-flourishing underground spring were dead.

A bare heel pounding on the side of the Rover was a signal to look up and see which new direction the bony finger was pointing.

"How much farther?" I asked.

The finger shook violently, urgently pointing the way. But the owner of the finger couldn't be bothered with idle chatter. When, two hours after the last direction, we hadn't heard anything from Lawrence, I reached up and grabbed his foot. He must have thought it was Zamba because he screamed, kicking my hand free, and nearly fell off the Rover.

"What! What! For the love of Allah!"

He had fallen asleep! The finger now urged us in another direction. His nap had cost us about an hour's driving.

We had been driving for most of the day, nonstop except for a couple of potty breaks, when we heard something fall off the top of the Rover, and a stream of clearly obscene Somali from behind us. When we came to a stop, we discovered Lawrence lying in the sand about a hundred yards to our rear. Apparently he had not only fallen asleep again, but had fallen off the roof as well! He walked toward us dusting off his clothes and cursing, but he had learned his lesson: he didn't fall asleep again.

Zamba may have had something to do with our guide's new-found alertness. Occasionally poor Lawrence's foot would slip down the side of the Rover, and Zamba liked to sniff it, and sometimes even take a lick. Lawrence would nearly jump out of his skin, letting out a pitiful yell.

We traveled all day into the interior, a wasteland of sand and rock. We saw no animals, no vegetation. But as the evening glow of the desert sun was slowly dropping beneath the ridge, there appeared an outcropping of large rocks and a patch of palm trees. In and around them were about a dozen striped tents. Situated in the middle was the inevitable camel well, bigger and sturdier than any we had seen so far. The scene was quiet and pleasant. An occasional camel bellowed, and some goats bleated. Camel bells chimed in the breeze, and tribal dialect could be heard coming from the tents.

The bare foot came down again and knocked against the Rover. I looked up and asked, "Where is . . . ?"

"Up there," came the response, as he pointed to a large, broad-striped tent blowing in the wind. "Mganga—but be ready for him not to see you."

As we came to a stop, Lawrence climbed down from the top of the Rover and spoke to a few men standing close by. With the draped window, no one could see Zamba. One of the men went into the tent and reappeared a few minutes later and spoke to Lawrence, who brought the news over to the car.

"He will not see you."

"Why?"

"You are infidels, white, and not of our kind. Let's go."

We had come so far! I was not to be discouraged, and urged him to try again, "Please tell him we have been driving for days just to meet him."

Lawrence shook his head. "We are lucky to have found him at all. We go."

"What is the hurry? Can't we at least stay the night, rest up before we head back?"

"No. We go now." He climbed back up on the car and pointed his long bony finger for us to get in.

I looked at Pip. She was as exhausted as I was. Then I had an idea.

"Lawrence, what did you tell him?"

"You wanted to speak to him. He said no."

"Did you mention Zamba?"

"No."

"Why not?"

"He said no!"

Going around to the back of the Rover, I undid the rear door and jumped Zamba out. The change in the distribution of weight almost dislodged Lawrence. The men in the camp saw Zamba, yelled, and ran in many directions.

"Lawrence, go tell the big Bwana that Zamba wants to see *him*."

"By Allah! He is sure very big much more outside of the car."

He slid down and entered the tent. We heard a few words, and then out came two Arab Askaris, holding the tent flap open for another man. He was an impressive person, quite tall, heavy, and bearded, wearing a white turban and many rings on each finger as well as a dozen or more necklaces. His *shuka* was a simple brown wrap thrown over another brownish wrap. A small pigsticker knife in a sheath was secured in his massive leather belt.

He approached Pippa and me slowly. His men put out their hands as a sign of caution, but he waved them away.

Apparently this was the Mganga. He stood looking at us, with an occasional glance at Zamba, who was relieving himself by a group of doom palm trees.

The Mganga wore a look of deep concentration. His thick dark eyebrows met at a point in the middle of his forehead. I figured he was trying his psychic powers on us. I may have been right.

Zamba had finished, and made his way to my side. He sat on his haunches and looked directly at the Mganga. I saw something I had seen him do before, on rare occasions, like his meeting with the blind girl, Dawn. Instead of looking at the medicine man, his eyes drifted to a point above him. There was a moment of tense, heavy silence, and then the Mganga gestured for us—me, Pippa, and the lion—to enter the tent.

The inside of the tent was filled with rugs, tapestries, brass pots, a pile of coconuts hanging from a camel saddle, a huge stack of figs, and a number of cups of fat with sisal pushed down into the muck for wicks. Masses of pillows were scattered throughout.

Lawrence followed us in and showed us where to sit. Zamba was given a large rug to lie on next to the entrance. For the next hour we spoke, through Lawrence, about many things. But whenever we asked a question regarding the Mganga's psychic abilities, he would answer it with another question that was totally unrelated. He wouldn't relinquish control of the conversation.

"How did you know you were able to read people's thoughts?" I asked.

"Where did you acquire the lion?" he asked back.

He wasn't completely closed to us. He told us how he lived, and where his family came from. After an hour he rose, his head nearly touching the top of the tent. He spoke to Lawrence, bowed his hands in a prayerful gesture, and left.

"What now?" I asked.

"You have been given a tent and food for the night. Tomorrow we will speak with him again."

The tent we were given was very comfortable. Food was brought: goat cheese, some strange and delicious fruits I had never seen before (or since), as well as figs, coconuts, and camel milk. We ate gratefully, and sleep came easily soon after. Zamba slept with us.

In the early morning, we were again called to sit cross-legged in the Mganga's tent. One of his men brought us some camel milk mixed with herbs and spices. The Mganga apparently had prepared himself for some sort of a reading. He looked for a few minutes at Zamba, who was busy licking his paws. I strained to see something in Zamba that was not there before, but I couldn't see anything special. I thought maybe I had hoped for too much.

But then, as the man stared at Zamba, my lion turned his head and again stared at the spot directly above his head. He did this for some time, and then unselfconsciously returned to his preening.

The Mganga sat cross-legged before us on the carpeted floor of the tent and spoke to Lawrence, who translated. "He has asked me to say exactly what he says. I must not interpret what he says, but repeat his exact words. What I speak—it will be as if he is speaking to you through me. So instead of 'he wants,' I'll say, 'I want.'

"You, as well, are not to interpret what I say. You are to listen exactly what my words are."

The Mganga leaned forward and looked us directly in the eye. His voice was deep and penetrating, and he spoke in a monotone. As I listened to Lawrence's voice and looked at the Mganga, a strange thing occurred. It was as though I could understand him, as though he were speaking English. I looked at Pippa and saw that she, too, was feeling the same thing. Lawrence's voice became the Mganga's voice, his words the Mganga's words.

This is what he said: "All that I will say, you will not believe, because you will not understand. And one must understand before he can believe."

He took out a beautiful container made of polished wood, and began to turn it in his hands. I could hear whatever was inside rattling around as it turned.

"I am one of ten brothers," the Mganga continued. "None of them has been able to do what I do. Many people have tried, none have succeeded. I do not know how I do what I do, nor why I am allowed to do it. I do know that what I do is true and real and is not to be questioned. If you sit with me, you must open your mind and heart, and in so doing, your spirit will come forth and tell you of what I say."

From the container he poured a few Arab beads into his hand, touching and rolling them between his fingers. He chose two from the ten or twelve in his hand and set the others in their own pile.

"Things come to me and I give them to you. If you do not want to know these truths, then you must leave now. Otherwise, all that I see will be spoken."

We had no doubt that we wanted to continue, although we had no idea what we would hear.

"Only when one distances himself from the world of noise and chaos can the mind hear the other side. The readings come from the earth around me, through me, not from me. They pass through me and I pick from them what I feel is important to have and give out. All of life is one. It is like a spider's web. When one thing disrupts the web, it is felt by all. I feel I must be a single thread in the web of the world. How else would I feel the vibrations?"

Again he poured more beads into his hand, felt them, and then separated a few out into the small pile.

"It will not be necessary for you to ask me any questions. They will be answered in due course."

After some time, a number of beads had accumulated in the small pile on the rug in front of him. The large pile he returned to the container and set aside. He rolled and touched the smaller group in his hands for the rest of the time we were in the tent.

As he rolled them, he spoke. "Each of these marbles carries the messages I am looking for. By rolling them in my hand, energy comes through clearly. Bwana, you and Pippa will not be together in the future. Your love for each other is strong, but another entity will separate you both in your early life."

Pippa gripped my hand tightly. That was not what we had planned. Tears came to her eyes.

"Ralph, you have an ability that few others have, but your life has too many other things happening in it to allow your greatness to come through. You seek to communicate with nature, but it will be hindered by the multitude of things that come into your life. You have a compassion for all life. It is an attribute but also a detriment.

"Zamba is a lion of the universe. He will not survive unless he is conditioned to cope with the knowledge you share with him in your life. The multitude of things in your life will hinder your ability to speak to one another.

"The communication you seek is within your grasp through him but your world is far too congested for you to hear him. Listen in the quiet places and maybe you will hear him. You will not speak in your tongue or his to hear each other. You will speak within yourselves to hear each other. Zamba knows not of what I say here today, but he feels it and knows the feeling and warmth coming from it.

"The communication you seek is found in the emotions of all living things, and in the energy of the earth. This is what you must learn to be able to speak to all things."

Each time the man made a significant statement, he dropped a bead into the container. Then he had one left. He looked at the bead, hesitated, and then dropped it into the bottle. What that bead represented, I will never know.

"What . . . ?"

He waved his hand and set the container down.

"I have welcomed you to my tent because of the unusual nature that you bring. Zamba and I are one."

For the first time he touched Zamba. He put his hand on his head and said a few Arabic words. Zamba's head was down, as if in sleep.

"*Inshallah.*" ("May God be with you.")

We bowed and thanked the man for his time and courtesy.

We asked to pay, but he refused, asking only that we take with us his profound thoughts and use them to better our lives.

Our Rover was loaded down with coconuts and figs. Palm fronds had been put on the roof and tied down to make shade for Zamba. A beautiful blanket was laid in the back for Zamba to lie on. Surely he had made an impression on the seer.

Pippa and I drove for hours in silence. It felt as if we were emerging from a trance. What had just happened? Were we hypnotized? Maybe. I only know that whatever it was had a traumatic effect on both of us. If we were to believe the Mganga, then we had to believe that we would not be together.

Zamba had no such qualms. He slept peacefully in the cool comfort of his palm-frond shelter.

27

 I returned to the States from Africa in 1963. I was a much wiser man for the trip, and vowed to get back to that continent as often as I could. The experience had a much more profound effect on me than I could ever have imagined. I had grown up in many ways during the trip, taking in a "spark of enlightenment" from everyone I had come into contact with. The openness of the land and people reaffirmed my belief in the importance of respect for life and nature.

As the Mganga had predicted, Pippa and I did in fact part ways, first when I came back to the States, and then again, in a much more permanent and devastating way than I ever could have imagined. About six weeks after I returned from Africa, I received a call. Pippa and a friend had been in an automobile accident. When the ambulance arrived with only enough room to take one person, Pippa had insisted that they take her friend. Waiting for them to return, she had a massive cerebral hemorrhage and died.

The news shocked me to my very core. My relationship with

Pippa had touched my life deeply, in every way. For me, she really did represent Africa and the possibilities of that continent. Devotion and love that deep don't dissipate easily. It took me a long time to get over the loss. I was depressed for months, and found it hard to put Pippa's death behind me.

But life's pull is very strong, especially when you're surrounded by animals, who remind you every day about the cycles of nature. Soon my world was again filled with blessings. The skies in the African nights hold the brightest of stars, and I believe that two of those stars followed me home and fell into my life when I returned to California. The first had been there before, however briefly. Just before I left for Africa, I had met Toni, and we had a short but very passionate relationship. Then, of course, I was gone for a year. But the whole time I was away, even despite the love I had felt for Pippa, Toni was never far from my thoughts.

It's pretty clear to me now that the trip to Africa enabled me to have a relationship with Toni. It gave me the maturity to see just how extraordinary she was, filled with some of the most wonderful contradictions. She had attended college, and modeled professionally, but she was equally as comfortable in cutoffs and dirty sneakers as she was in her evening gowns. She was highly spiritual, and could hold her own in conversation with some of the most learned religious scholars. Most impressive to me was her tremendous kindness and compassion, which allowed her to empathize completely with the exotic animals we lived and worked with.

Eventually, some time after I returned, I asked Toni to be my wife. She came to me at a time when I was in need of someone to gather in the reins of my runaway spirit, to slow me to a more tempered pace, and I credit her with guiding me through a time of tremendous, although sometimes difficult, growth.

The second star was my daughter with Toni, a child named

Tana, after a river in Kenya. She was, and is, one of the greatest blessings God has bestowed on me, and I feel that she, like her mother, was brought to earth to share her life with animals. She inherited her mother's beauty, inner and outer, and her incredible smile immediately transmits her love of life to everyone—animal or human—who comes in contact with her.

From the very beginning, Tana and Zamba had a special relationship. My relationship with Zamba was so close and so trusting that I never even thought twice about bringing my daughter up around him. Zamba knew lots of baby animals, and he always treated Tana with the utmost gentleness and respect. He'd never lick her skin, for instance, only her clothes, as if he knew that his rough tongue would hurt her. And I never saw his claws out when he was anywhere near her. They grew up together as siblings, and indeed, Tana called him her brother.

Needless to say, many people still can't believe I let them spend time together. Animals are dangerous around children. Children are unpredictable. They're small, they run around, and they have high-pitched voices—just like prey. To this day, Zamba is the only lion I've ever known whom I could imagine trusting with a child. But trust him I did. They used to watch television together— cartoons or Westerns—after dinner. She would curl up against him with a bowl of popcorn and drift off. My heart was filled with happiness to see them together like that; it was like beauty and the beast, except to me they were both beautiful.

Tana grew up to be an actress and stuntwoman in her own right. I'm sure a lot of people would accuse me of irresponsibility and child endangerment now. I'm sure that there are those who say that I was naïve at best, and dangerously crazy at worst, to bring my daughter up in a house with a lion. All I can say in my defense is that none of us ever really thought about it. Zamba was my son, the way Tana is my daughter. I never looked at him and saw teeth and claws and menace, in the same way that I never saw him as a pet. He was my friend, and a member of the family, and we lived in Camelot.

Tana's upbringing was—to say the least—unusual. She was probably one of the only children in the world who had a lion around as other kids had a family dog. It was not uncommon to see her riding on his back around the ranch.

Tana came home from school one day in tears; she had been reprimanded and sent to the principal's office for telling tall tales. Except, of course, in Tana's case, the tall tales were true. She *had* fallen asleep in bed with her parents—and a lion. There *was* a chimpanzee pulling her pigtails during dessert. The school suspended her, and told her not to come back until she was ready to be truthful. I was so furious that I loaded her and our beautiful elephant Modoc into a trailer and drove right back to the school. They talked about Tana parading around the parking lot on top of that elephant for years to come, and nobody ever accused her of lying again.

Sometimes I joke around, saying that Tana was raised using affection training as well—but it's only half a joke. In my experience, all young living things benefit when boundaries are enforced sensitively, and with compassion. I also feel sometimes that Tana, growing up as she did in loving communication and harmony with other species, is a more highly evolved human being as a result. At any rate, I am not sure how much her unconventional upbringing had to do with the beautiful vibrant, energetic, warm-hearted woman she became—but I wouldn't change a thing.

The Mganga was right about something else. My life was too busy, too cluttered, too filled with noise for me to hear the sounds I really craved, true communication with nature. But it would be a while before I would be able to silence the chatter.

28

Once back from Africa, Zamba was once again a regular on the studio lots, and the successful release of *The Lion* only increased his fame. He worked steadily and consistently in commercials, movies, and television. For instance, Zamba was the lion in all the Tarzan films after Johnny Weismuller stopped doing them—the Tarzans kept changing, but the lion was the same!

His next major star turn was as Fluffy in the movie of the same name, with Tony Randall and Shirley Jones. Shirley had won a well-deserved Oscar for her role in *Elmer Gantry* a few years before, and proved an absolute treat to work with. She and Zamba had a very special relationship, and one that continued long after filming.

My own career was at a peak. I'd spent twelve years struggling to get to the top, and I finally felt that I'd made it. We were doing a lot of lucrative, high-profile work. It was 1966. I had just completed shooting *Gentle Ben,* as well as the television show *The Greatest Show on Earth,* with Jack Palance, in which Zamba featured prominently. The television show *Daktari* was being filmed at our ranch. We had fifteen hundred wild animals there, and a crew of dedicated keepers and trainers.

The ranch was beautiful. Nestled at the bottom of Soledad Canyon, about thirty miles north of Los Angeles, the property snaked for a mile down the canyon beside the banks of the Santa Clarita stream. The highway wound above it on one side, the railroad track on the other.

Zamba, like many of our animals, made regular appearances on *Daktari*. Judy the chimp had more regular hours than an accountant, and her own director's chair. Filming went on for four years, and by the end of it, the assistant directors had forgotten that she wasn't a human actor. "Judy, you're up in five," they'd say.

It seemed that all my hard work had paid off. I was comfortable financially, for the first time in my life. My affection-based system for working with animals dominated the industry—finally, cruelty was no longer the norm. I had a beautiful wife and a terrific daughter. My life seemed to be running without a hitch, and I finally felt as if I could stop and take a breather.

Then, at the beginning of the year, the rain started. And it wouldn't stop. It rained for weeks—sometimes heavily, with thunder and lightning, and sometimes just a mist of light rain. But it was always there, and over the course of a month or two, the blankets, the beds, and the whole house were constantly damp.

We'd had heavy rains before, and even a few floods, but nothing we couldn't handle. There was a flood-control dam above us, fifteen miles up the canyon, and we weren't too worried about the stream overflowing. Just to make sure, we had asked the city's flood control office for advice when we moved in. They checked their records for the biggest flood in a hundred-year history, and calculated that to handle one that size we would need a channel one hundred feet wide, twelve feet deep, and one mile long. It cost us one hundred thousand dollars and three months of hard work, but we built it. It was worth it to feel safe.

One day during the endless rain, Toni, Zamba, and I were doing our morning rounds to make sure our animals were dry and safe. Toni went over to check on the "wild string," a group of lions, tigers, bears, and leopards that had been donated to us by people who never should have had them in the first place. Although we knew that very few spoiled mature animals could ever be indoctrinated with affection training, we had taken them in—hopeless animal lovers can be suckers.

I checked at the office for messages, then Zamba and I headed for "Beverly Hills," our nickname for the area where our movie-star animals lived—Gentle Ben, Clarence the cross-eyed lion, Judy the chimp, Bullfrog the "talking" buffalo, Modoc the elephant, and many others.

The rain had become a steady downpour by the time we were finished there, and Zamba's mane was getting soaked, which he hated. It was at the rhino enclosure that I began to worry a little, when I noticed that I could no longer jump over the stream that ran beside their barn.

The sky was now opening up with a vengeance. I threw my poncho over Zamba, tied it around his neck to keep the rain out, and continued my tour of inspection. I wanted to finish up as quickly as I could, then find some shelter.

I was just wondering how Toni was making out with the wild string when my head trainer, Frank Lamping, arrived. He told me that the earthen dam above us was about to go. To prevent the dam from bursting, the flood control people were opening the floodgates to release the pressure. We were to watch out for some heavy water coming downstream.

The inspection took on urgency, and word went out to the crew to redouble our efforts. Anything that needed to be done to make the ranch safe needed to be done *now*. I told Frank to check the stock area, and a trainer yelled from the roadway above that he had the nursery section under control.

I used a small cord that I found near the barn to tie Zamba to a small tree.

"Just for a little while," I told him.

He didn't like to be tethered, but I felt I could move faster if I was sure he was staying in one place. The rain was beginning to erode the supports underneath the elephant barn, so I set to digging a channel to divert the flow of water away from the barn.

I was working hard, looking down at my shovel, when I heard a low roar, coming louder and closer. Startled, I looked behind me, and suddenly there it was—a solid wall of water. To this day, I have never seen anything like it. It must have been thirty feet high, and it was carrying with it a frightening amount of debris, including full-sized oak trees and a couple of sheds.

That was all the warning I got before I saw it hit. Down it came, crashing and exploding against the compound, uprooting cages, overturning buildings and trucks—anything in its way. Fortunately, Zamba and I were on high ground, just above the spot the tidal wave hit, or we would unquestionably have been swept away.

Instantly, everything was in chaos. Sheer panic broke out among the animals in the Beverly Hills section. Lions were roaring and hitting against the sides of their cages; bears were lunging against the bars; chimps were screaming. The water was starting to rock the cages. Some were already floating and were about to be swept downstream.

I could hardly believe my eyes, but there wasn't time for calcula-tion. It was impossible to determine where my efforts would do the most good. I raced for the cages, but was thrown down by the weight of the water, which was all the way up to my chest. Miguel, one of our dedicated keepers, came running over to help, yelling half in English and half in Spanish. I told him to grab a large coil of rope that was hanging in a tree nearby, and to hold one end. I fastened the other end around myself and started out into the filthy, freezing water. If I could just get to the cages, I could unlock the doors and set the animals free. At least then they could fend for themselves—it was their only chance. Otherwise they'd all drown, trapped in their cages.

The water was rushing past me furiously. I struggled through it to Gentle Ben's cage, fumbling on my ring for the key. "For Chrissake, don't *drop* it!" I pleaded with myself. With shaking hands, I got the key turned in the lock, and threw open the door.

The great old bear landed right on top of me in his panicked race for freedom. There was nothing to do but to grab his heavy coat and hang on, as his massive body carried me over to a group of cages holding more than twenty animals. The water was now five or six feet deep. Cages were starting to come loose from their foundations; the animals were swimming inside them, fighting for breath.

I let go of Ben and grabbed on to the steel bars of one of the cages. My heart sank as I saw Ben dog-paddling, trying unsuccessfully to reach the embankment. I could just barely make out his form as he was carried through some rough white water and around a bend before he was lost from my view.

But there was no time, no time. One by one I released the animals—leopards, tigers, bears—talking as calmly as I could, even managing an occasional pat or kiss of farewell. It was a testament to their training that they trusted me enough to jump into the freezing, filthy water, and I watched, sick and helpless, as they were carried away, swept along with the torrent of water. Some would come together for a moment only to be whisked away again, as though a giant hand shoved them. Some went under. I strained to see whether any of them came up again, but it was impossible to tell.

My wonderful, beloved animals were fighting for their lives.

Word came down to me that Toni and Tana were all right, and Toni had joined the rescue efforts. With my human family safe, I was free to focus again on the animals. To my right, about thirty feet out in the water and half submerged, was a large, heavy steel cage on wheels with a row of four compartments in it. I managed to get to it just as the force of the current started to move it. I began to open the compartments, one by one, but the cage began to move faster downstream, carrying me with it. I looked back to the shore at Miguel. He saw the problem and threw his end of the rope around a large tree branch. We were running out of time. If the rope came to the end of its slack before I could get it off me and onto the cage, we would lose the cage. It was picking up speed, and the animals inside were roaring and barking in terror. I decided to hold the cage myself, with the rope tied around my waist.

There were two beautiful wolves in the last cage, Sheba and Rona. Toni and I had raised them since they were pups. I was at their door, fumbling with the lock, when the rope locked taut around me. I thought it would cut me in half. I grabbed the steel bars with both hands, leaving the key in the lock, praying it wouldn't drop out. But when I reached down once more to open the lock, a rush of water knocked the key out of the lock and into the torrent.

I was completely stunned. I knew I had just signed those animals' death warrants. The water behind the cage was building up, pushing against it with a wall of incredible force. I held on as tightly as I could for as long as I could, but eventually the cage was ripped out of my hands.

I fell backward into the churning water, and when I surfaced, I could see the cage out in the main stream, racing with the trees, bushes, and building debris, heading on down the raging river. Sheba and Rona seemed almost calm. My tears joined the flood as my beloved friends were washed away.

By this time, it had become clear to me what had happened. The floodgates on the dam had been opened, all right, but because the ground was already saturated with the thirty inches of rain that had fallen in the last few weeks, it couldn't absorb any more. And the new storm had hit at the same time, dumping another fourteen inches on us in twenty-four hours. Together, these conditions had caused this horrendous flood.

I would find out later that it was the largest flood that had been recorded in that area—ever. We were really hard hit, because the water had been held up occasionally on its fifteen-mile journey down the canyon by debris in its path. This allowed huge amounts of water to fill up behind the logjams, doubling the force of the flood when released. By the time the water reached us, huge waves had built up; the water and debris came crashing down on us like a tidal wave, then subsided, only to come crashing down again, over and over.

We were to struggle through two days and nights of unbelievable havoc and terror, trying desperately to salvage what we could of the ranch.

I scrambled my way to the embankment, concerned for Zamba. I saw a high and dry area that the river had not yet reached. I grabbed his lead and we started to cross over, but were immediately carried downstream by the current and pulled into a whirlpool. I grabbed Zamba's mane, and together we swam for the safety of the shore. After resting a bit, I managed to get back to the main area, high above the flood line, leaving him in as good a spot as any. At least for the moment, he was safe. I tied him up with the small cord.

"Stay here, Zamba."

He gave a moan, and it was clear that he wanted to go with me, but he was better off keeping to the high ground.

The storm grew worse. Heavy sheets of rain filled and overflowed our flood channel, undermining its sides until they caved in. By midmorning the Santa Clarita River had become a raging, murderous torrent, a hundred fifty feet wide and fifteen feet deep, moving through Africa U.S.A. with the speed and force of an express train. In its fury it wiped out a two-lane highway, full-grown oak trees, generator buildings—everything. Our soundstage was in a full-sized building, one hundred feet long by fifty feet wide, but the water just picked it up like a matchbox and carried it away downstream, end over end, rolling it like a toy and depositing it on a sand embankment a mile away. Electric wires flared brightly as the water hit them. We rushed for the main switch to the soundstage, shutting everything down in the fear that somebody would be electrocuted.

You don't think at a time like that—you *do*. My people risked their lives over and over again for the animals. We'd be half drowned and make our way to the shore just long enough to clear our lungs before heading back out into the water.

The waves hit the elephant pens next, and they hit them hard. We moved the elephants out just as the building collapsed and was carried downstream. Then the waves caught the camels' cage, pulling it into the water. One huge camel was turning over and over as he was swept along. Sometimes black humor is the only thing that gets you through a moment like that. I thought crazily, *If that camel drowns, will some future archaeologist dig up its bones and say, "My God, there must have been camels in Los Angeles!"?*

We worked in a frenzy. Animals were everywhere. Bears, lions, and tigers were jumping out of their cages, only to be swept downstream. Saving them was no easy task. They were either hanging on to our legs and pulling us under, or we were hanging on to them and swimming for shore.

I unlocked the cheetah's cage and he sprang out over my head, right into the water, and was gone. I remember grabbing hold of Serang, one of our Bengal tigers, as he came out of his cage. He carried me on his back to temporary security on the opposite bank as smoothly as if we'd rehearsed it.

I worked without a break, Zamba always at the back of my mind. I knew he was up on a dry spot—but I also knew that no dry spot was a guaranteed haven for very long under these conditions. I managed to work my way around the debris and forged across the tributary the river had formed to get to the spot where I had left him.

I wouldn't have thought that there was any energy left in my battered body for shock or grief, but there was. A huge oak tree had crashed onto the area where I had told him to stay. The water was backed up a good six feet deep, and Zamba was gone.

"Zamba! Zamba!" I screamed his name against the roar of the flood but there was no answer. Zamba was gone. He was a fairly good swimmer, but I knew his mane could weigh him down and hold his head under the water.

I shuttered my mind to the thought that he had drowned. Grief was a luxury I didn't have time for; action was my only option, so I swallowed my panic and kept looking. Everybody was busy, searching for life and saving any animal he could find. There was no one to help me look for Zamba. I searched everywhere I could, calling his name at the top of my lungs. I couldn't believe he was gone. I envisioned him lying somewhere hurt, needing me.

As the storm continued, the river was full of animals and people swimming together. There was no "kill" instinct in operation, only that of survival. Men were grabbing fistfuls of fur, clinging for life. A monkey grabbed a lion's tail, which allowed him to make it to safety.

I saw that Clarence the cross-eyed lion was in a complete state of panic. The river had surrounded him and was now flooding his cage. His trainer, Bob, waded across the water, put a chain on Clarence, took him out of his cage, and attempted to jump him across the raging stream. But the lion wouldn't jump. The water was rising rapidly. There was no time for niceties. Bob threw his body weight against the chain, trying to drag Clarence out if he wouldn't go of his own accord. It wasn't working—the lion was simply too big. So Bob threw part of the chain to me. To gain some leverage, I looped it around a pipe running alongside a building. As we both pulled, Clarence finally jumped, and just then the pipe I was holding on to came loose. It turned out to be a "hot" electric conduit, for when Clarence leaped and the pipe came loose, we all got a tremendous electric shock! Fortunately the pipe also pulled the wires loose, so the shock lasted only an instant. Had it continued, it would certainly have killed us, as we were standing knee-deep in water.

With Clarence safe, Bob and I noticed a group of monkeys trapped in a small outcropping of dirt and debris in the middle of the river. Another trainer, Frank, almost died trying to save them; he tied a rope around his waist and started across, but about halfway over he slipped and went under. We finally saw him in midstream, trying to stay afloat. We didn't know what to do, whether to pull on the rope or not, because it seemed that whenever we pulled on the rope, he would go under. (We found out later that the rope had become tangled around his foot; every time we yanked it, we pulled him under.) We ended up taking an enormous risk and cutting the rope altogether. He made it, thank God, and he was able to swim the animals to safety.

We were racing against time. The river was still rising, piling up uprooted trees and parts of buildings and pushing them along in front, forming a wall of destruction. Throughout the turmoil and strife, one thing was crystal clear to me: without affection training, all would have been lost. It was extraordinary to see it working under such horrendous circumstances. As dangerous and frightening as this emergency was, these animals remained calm enough to let themselves be led to safety when it was possible for us to do so.

The wild string panicked, and in their hysteria they attacked their rescuers as if they were enemies. In the end, we had to resort to tranquilizer guns. We fired darts into each fear-trained animal, and as they succumbed to the medication, we held their bodies up above the water and carried them to safety. Tragically, there was not enough time to drag all of them to safety; several drowned in their drugged sleep before we could reach them.

Imagine yourself in a raging storm, with buildings crashing alongside of you. You make your way to a cage that houses a lion or a tiger, and the animal immediately understands why you're there and is happy to see you. You open the door, put a leash on the animal, and you both jump out into the freezing, swirling water. Together you're swept down the stream, hitting logs, rolling over and over, as you try to keep your arms around the animal. Together you get up onto the safety of dry land. You dry off, give your animal a big hug, and then go back in for another one.

Chimpanzees are deathly afraid of water, because they can't

close their noses as humans can, and they know that they're dead if their heads go under. But even the chimps were trusting their human companions to take them to safety, voluntarily jumping into the freezing waters. It seemed a terrible, terrible irony that this was the circumstance under which my dream—of true communication between man and beast—would be realized.

There was one big cage left in the back section containing a lion. This lion was a killer who had been fear-trained; we had taken him in because he had nowhere else to go. A group of us went out to him. The other lions were being saved because we could swim with them, but this fellow was too rough. I got to the cage and opened the door. A couple of my men threw ropes on the lion and pulled, trying to get him out of his potential grave—but he wouldn't come out. He was petrified! We pulled and struggled and fought to get him out of the cage, but we couldn't do it, and we finally had to let him go.

The storm continued on into the night, and with the darkness came a nightmare of confusion. We worked on without sleep, sustained by coffee and desperation. My thoughts of Zamba came hard and fast, but I did my best to push them away to the periphery. There wasn't anything I could do for him now. I would work where I was needed.

During that night, it became clear that ancient Modoc the elephant, the one-eyed wonder of the big top, had by no means outlived her capacity for calmness and courage in the face of disaster. Modoc took over, understanding fully what was at stake and what was required of her. Animal after animal was saved as she labored at the water's edge, hauling cages to safety on higher ground. When the current tore a cage free and washed it downstream, Modoc got a firmer grip on the rope with her trunk, and with the power of several bulldozers, steadily dragged the cage back to safety. Then a trainer would attach the rope to another endangered pen, and Modoc would resume her labors. She was astonishingly brave and wise, and she had many rescues to her credit that night.

We eventually became stranded with some of the animals on an "island," a patch of high ground in the middle of the compound. This, plus an area alongside the railroad track, was all that was left of Africa U.S.A. When the dam had burst upstream, the wall of water that hit the ranch divided into two fast-moving rivers. As time passed, the rivers widened and deepened until they were impossible to cross. As dusk fell on the second day, we realized that we were cut off from the mainland. Since it was the highest ground on the ranch, the island in the center had become a haven for all the survivors. The office building, the vehicles, and about twenty cages were all well above the flooded zone, and so were safe for the time being. The giraffes, some monkeys, and one lion were all housed in makeshift cages on the island.

A railroad track ran behind the office building. By following the tracks for three miles, it would be possible to reach the highway. The problem would then be crossing the torrent of water to get to the road.

I noticed that Bullfrog, our thousand-pound Indian buffalo, was gone. Buffalos are known to be excellent swimmers, and I had thought for sure that he would have made it to safety. I asked around to learn whether anyone had seen him. No one had. Bullfrog's cage had always been at the entrance to the ranch, because he greeted visitors with a most unusual bellow that sounded exactly like the word "hi." Now he was gone, too. Would it ever end? I felt weak. The temperature had dropped, and the wind had come up. The wind-chill factor was now below zero.

There's something especially horrible about tragedy that occurs in the dark. I could hear the water running behind me, and every once in a while I'd hear a big timber go, or an animal cry, or a person shouting. It all seemed very surreal.

Throughout the night and all the next day the rain continued, and we worked on. Luckily, help came from everywhere. The highway, which we could no longer get to but which we could see, was lined with cars. Some people had successfully rigged up a bos'n chair, a winch with a body harness fifty feet in the air, and were sending hot food and drink over to us, a distance of some two hundred yards. Other people were walking three miles over the hills to bring supplies. A citizens-band club set up radio communication. The actor Gardner McKay, a true friend, put his Mercedes on the railway track, deflated the tires, and slowly drove down to help us. One elderly woman prepared ham and coffee and brought it in at two o'clock in the morning, only to find on her return that her car had been broken into and robbed!

Then a train engine came down the track to help—just an engine, no cars. The electricity, of course, was out all over the ranch, which left the reptiles especially vulnerable, as they need warmth to survive. Three girls from our affection-training school volunteered to rescue the snakes. They climbed onto the cowcatcher, the metal grill on the front of the engine. We then wrapped about thirty feet of python and boa constrictor around their shoulders and told them where to take the snakes once they were on the other side. Goats, aoudads, and llamas all rode in the coal bin behind the engine. I'll never forget the look on one girl's face as the engine pulled out and a python crawled through her hair.

By four the next morning, some twenty people had, by one method or another, made it over to our island to help. Some chose a dangerous way, tying ropes around their middles and entering the water slowly, with friends on the island holding the other ends of the ropes. The current would carry them quickly downstream, and they would look for a logjam or boulder to stop them so they could make their way to where we were.

I was having some coffee in the watchmen's trailer when the scream of an animal shattered the night. I dashed out to find a small group of people huddled together, trying to find the animal with their flashlights. We could hear it desperately struggling in the raging water. It had succeeded in swimming out of the turbulence at the middle of the stream, but the sides of the river were too slippery for it to get a foothold and climb to safety. The noise and the darkness made it impossible for us to figure out which animal it was.

Then I heard it: "Hi! Hi!" It was a call of desperation from Bullfrog the buffalo, as he fought for his life. There was nothing we could do to help him, and his "hi's" trailed down the dark, black abyss, fading as he was carried away around the bend.

Then Toni screamed at me in the dark, "Ralph, over here!" I fought my way through a maze of debris and water and burst into a clearing. There was Toni, holding a flashlight on—lo and behold—a big steel cage from Beverly Hills! It had been washed downstream and was lodged in the trunk of a toppled tree. It was still upright, but its back was facing us, and we couldn't see inside. We waded out to the cage. Toni kept calling, "Sheba, Rona, are you there? Please answer!" Our hearts were beating fast, and Toni was crying.

Hoping against hope that the wolves were still alive, we rounded the corner, half swimming and half falling. Then we eased up to the front of the cage and looked straight into two sets of the most beautiful eyes I'd ever seen. Rona and Sheba had survived! They practically jumped out of their skins when they saw us, as though to say, "Is it really *you?*" Toni had her key, and we unlocked the door. Both wolves fell all over us, knocking us into the water. They couldn't stop licking our faces and whimpering.

The rain finally let up on the morning of the third day. The sun came out, and at last we had time to stop, look around, and assess the damage. It was devastating, and heartrending.

Most of the animals had been let out of their cages and had totally disappeared, including Judy the chimp, Clarence the lion, Pajama Tops the zebra, and Raunchy, our star jaguar. We knew a few others had definitely drowned. Both of the white rhinos were missing, and so were the hippos. Our beloved Gentle Ben had been washed away, along with hundreds of other animals. Zamba was nowhere to be found. Every time someone screamed that he had found an animal, my heart jumped. Was it Zamba?

I was sitting there looking at the wreckage when somebody put a cup of hot chocolate in my hand. It was Toni. Her clothes were torn and wet, hair slicked her to her head, lips blue from the cold. What a woman! Earlier, she had managed to make her way to the nursery where all the baby animals were quartered. Without exception, the babies had followed her to safety. Not one baby animal had been lost.

The hot liquid felt good going down. I stood up and hugged Toni, and we walked arm in arm. The sun was just topping the cottonwoods, and the river had subsided. All was quiet, except for an occasional animal noise: a yelp, a growl, a snort. All the animals were happy to see the sun, to feel its warmth.

Toni and I felt only the heavy, leaden feeling of loss. During the storm, all we had been able to think about was the loss of animal life, the tragedy we were witnessing. Now, in the harsh light of day, I realized that I was seeing ten years of my life go down the drain as well. Our home, across the street, was safe, but our business was essentially destroyed. We had just signed a contract with Universal Studios to open our beautiful ranch to their tours; this would now be impossible. A million dollars was gone, maybe more. But still, all these calculations paled in the face of the loss of some of our beloved animals.

We turned around to head back to the temporary camp. So many people were there at the ranch! We were once again connected with the rest of the world. Exhausted, wet, wonderful people—true heroes, animal lovers every one. They had come from everywhere. Some were employees, some friends, and some strangers, but everyone greeted us as we came down the hill with expressions of hope and love on their faces. They cared, and it showed.

The animals were out of crisis, but they couldn't stay in the state they were in. The work was only just beginning, as one by one, we fed, cleaned, and housed them as best we could.

"Ralph, come quickly!" screamed a voice. "He made it, he made it! *He's alive!*"

"Who, who?" I screamed, scrambling toward the sound. Immediately I heard a resounding "Hi, hi!" From around the corner came Bullfrog—disheveled and muddy, but alive!

"Hi, hi!"

"Yes, *hi,* you big, lovable . . . Hi! Hi!"

Everyone pitched in for the massive cleanup effort. Animals were straining to pull big trucks out of the water and muck. Bakery trucks were coming by with stale bread for the elephants. Farmers loaned us their bulldozers to round up the hippos and rhinos. (One hippo fell in love with the skip-loader bucket and coyly followed it home.) Our neighbors—even people who had suffered terrible damage to their own homes—were amazing, lending us anything they could spare. Charley and Madeline Franks, two loyal helpers, kept hot chili coming, and must have dished out hundreds of meals. People from the Humane Society, Fish and Game, Animal Regulation, and the SPCA all helped to comfort and tend the animals.

We began searching for the animals that were still lost. Everyone was busy constructing makeshift cages. The medical lab trailer was pulled out of the mud. The nursery building and its kitchen storage area had been completely submerged, and some of it had been washed away. Whatever could be salvaged was taken up to the island for immediate use.

Outside the ranch, the animals began turning up everywhere. The police informed us that elephants had shown up in people's backyards. Eagles sat in the limbs of suburban trees. Llamas and guanacos cruised the local restaurants, and monkeys were spotted in parking lots. In no case was there a problem between an animal and people.

We had had dozens of alligators, some weighing two hundred to three hundred pounds. They had suffered real tragedy—we lost most of them because the ice-cold water had hit the whole pen, and it battered and beat them mercilessly. For seven months afterward we'd read in the paper that the bodies of alligators were being found everywhere, up to forty-five miles away. There were helicopter and airplane photos of alligators that had been killed, their bodies lying in the sand as the water subsided.

As the cleanup efforts progressed, I was starting to feel the full shock of everything that had happened. But, other than the alligators, the overall animal loss had been much less terrible than we'd imagined. Of the fifteen hundred animals we'd had at Africa U.S.A., only nine had drowned. Five of those were animals that had not been affection trained. But our other losses had been enormous, and my beloved Zamba was still at large, as was Gentle Ben. With a heavy heart, I had gone back again and again to the area where I had last seen Zamba. I thought that maybe the big tree had hit and killed him, but his body was nowhere to be found.

As the emergency lessened and mopping-up operations took

over, I felt worse and worse. The shakes set in, and I developed a high fever. The doctors said it was walking pneumonia, and that rest, good food, and warmth were in order. But there were still too many things to do, and now was not the time to stop.

I did, however, need to find a place to sit down and relax. I found a log in a quiet spot, away from the main cleanup efforts. As soon as I sat down and allowed myself to stop, my body began to tremble with shock, as well as illness. The combination of pneumonia, emotional pain, and sheer physical exhaustion spelled overload. I just couldn't handle any more. I had no more tears. I was numb. I sat in the middle of the chaos with an old blanket wrapped around me, unmoving, unable to give any more orders.

I had closed my eyes and was drifting off to sleep when something warm and wet on my face woke me up. I opened my eyes and saw Ben's big wise face right next to mine. *Gentle Ben had come home!!* I hugged him and cried like a baby.

I turned to get up to tell everyone, but I didn't have to. They were all there. Toni and a big group of the others had brought him to me. He'd been found two miles down the canyon, mud-covered and a few pounds lighter, but safe! Tears were in everybody's eyes—it even seemed that old Ben's eyes were glistening.

Toni saw the state I was in and suggested that we take a little walk together up to our favorite ridge above the railroad track. It was a short walk uphill, on a winding trail that led up to a glorious meadow scattered with sycamore and cottonwood trees. From there you could see forever. We had gone there many times in the evening to wish the sun good night and sometimes to give a welcome to a new moon. As we approached the hill, we could see that the rain had brought out a million different kinds of flowers, which blanketed the hills for miles around.

A prism in the sky caught my eye, arching across the ravaged countryside. I practically laughed out loud. This had been a time in my life when I felt I had reached the end of the rainbow. I had touched the pot of gold, had dug my hand deep into happiness and prosperity. But it was fool's gold, a fleeting pleasure. Suddenly, all that I had created was gone. I hadn't realized how vulnerable the world is, how delicate the balance of forces that sustain our existence.

A slight breeze carried the many animal sounds from the ranch below up to us.

Then, very faintly, I heard a noise I'd recognize anywhere.

"Augh!"

It was the greeting sound of a lion.

"Did you hear that?" I asked Toni.

"I did," she said. "Oh! My God, I did." Tears were welling up in her eyes.

Again, the "augh!" Following the sound, we broke into a run. And when we got to the top of the hill, a sight greeted us that neither one of us will ever forget. Nestled under those cottonwood trees was a vision of the Peaceable Kingdom.

Lying together in the sun were camels, a llama, a baby hippo, an eland, a few deer, a swarm of ducks and geese, a few tigers and cougars. We stood awestruck. It was truly an incredible sight; both of us felt we were witnessing a miracle, living a moment in history. The animals, tattered and bedraggled, were grooming and grazing and acting as if nothing at all was out of the ordinary. It was a totally impossible scene, one out of a movie, or a children's storybook. Animals that should have been enemies sharing turf without strife! Mammals were lying down unconcernedly with carnivores. It was like the Garden of Eden must have been. Affection training had taken a far greater leap than I could have ever imagined. These animals must have fought their way clear of the treacherous waters and, one by one, climbed the hill, slept, and dried off together in the morning sun. They hadn't run away, or fought among themselves. In fact, they seemed to be waiting for us. The lamb could truly lie down with the lion, without fear

And, right in the center, the most beautiful lion in the whole world.

ZAMBA! My Zamba.

Zamba met us halfway, and we smothered each other with hugs and kisses. He was limping, and I immediately saw the problem: a deep slash on his right front leg. I tried to look at the cut but he turned away, and I felt sure that the injury was deep.

"It's okay, boy—we'll attend to that when we get home."

I felt proud and humble among the animal dignitaries, and, for the first time, self-conscious in front of Zamba. He really was a god of nature; his mane was a crown, one given only to those worthy to carry it.

Toni and I descended to the ranch below, with Zamba limping at my side. Behind him came a long line of animals: camels, a llama, hippo, eland, cougars—all wound their way down the trail to the ranch below. I periodically checked behind me, staggered by what I was seeing. It was a phenomenal, biblical vision: they had been waiting for us to take them home.

In the distance I could see the sky clearing, and I thought that someday there would be another rainbow, its treasure waiting for me. Until then, we had a job to do. We needed to start all over again.

29

It was the eighteenth anniversary of the day Brini and Jack had left that burlap-covered cage with me, years after the storm that had almost taken Zamba away from me. And, as we had done many, many times before, Zamba and I were going up the trail to visit the Old Lady.

The summer showers had turned the forest and canyons into a sea of waving emerald. The rich scent of sage and pungent pine in the valley's thick undergrowth wafted up to us as Zamba and I climbed our way along the narrow twisting trail. He was off his leash, walking freely, with my hand resting gently on his shoulders. His mane lay soft and thick underneath my hand. Any light breeze would blow it across his forehead, like a schoolboy who has forgotten to comb his hair. Streaks of silver hair were now intertwined with the red and gold.

The early morning mist hung along the fringe of the thicket, disturbed only by the occasional flutter of wings above us. Zamba's huge, soft pads, so quiet, seemed to barely touch the earth. The breezes at the top of the pines, the mountain springs bubbling down into the valley, and the various bird songs made the forest seem loud.

As we walked together, I talked to him. He stared straight ahead, sometimes answering me with a groan. I teased him: "Why don't lions like people who are chatterboxes?" and he bumped up against my leg but kept going. He was a good listener. If I ever got a little philosophical, he would just stop, give me his full attention for a long minute, and then keep walking. I don't know how he could separate my nonsense chatter from other, more creative thoughts—probably my intonation. It did make him a good audience, though, better than most of the humans I know.

Zamba seemed tired. His breathing was labored, and when we stopped at one of the switchbacks to rest a bit, he settled down, leaning his body against my leg. Maybe we should have driven, I thought, but the way of the trail was a far more precious experience.

This was the trail on which as a cub, Zam had raced ahead, then peered around the bend to see if I was still coming. Sometimes I hid behind a tree until he came looking for me. The noise he made then was the same noise a lion would make when calling for his kin. I would wait until he was almost upon me, and then I'd leap out at him. He would jump away, faking fear and surprise, racing around in circles and leaping into the air with such exuberance that the birds and squirrels would scatter.

But the animals no longer ran from him. Even the deer stopped foraging the green grass and stood motionless as he passed, as though they knew him. Maybe some of them remembered being chased by him as a cub.

I stroked his head gently. His eyes closed at the touch. "It's better to go slow, old man," I said. "You get to see more." So we rested every so often, picking the best spots to take in the view below.

We reached the Old Lady just before dusk. She stood as proud and beautiful as ever, although some of her outer branches had fallen and turned brown, reminding me of someone whose temples have turned gray.

Zamba and I went to our rock, a giant piece of granite that lay at the edge of a precipice looking out at the quiet forest below. We heard the caw of ravens and the shrieks of a red-tailed hawk. Was it the same hawk that I had seen when we first met? I wondered.

Zamba was sitting sphinxlike on the rock overlooking the forest, but his eyes were closed. Where was he? I wondered. Visiting his youth? Was he remembering Africa? Or was he just getting old and tired? I felt a pang—had he come on this journey just to please me? It would be like him. So many times in our lives together, he had thought of me first.

The sun began to set, always spectacular from this vantage point, the colors like those in Zamba's mane. So we sat together, with my arm wrapped around his shoulders, and I found tears streaming down my face. My life with Zamba had been an even greater experience than I had dared to imagine it would be. He had given me such happiness, and he had been such a good teacher, allowing me into his world and showing me the ways of nature. I ached with love for him.

The colors of the sunset were changing rapidly, scarlet meshing with dark violet, and the hint of an evening chill drifted up from the valley below. I wiggled my fingers deeper into his fur, each of us comforted by the other's warmth. As the purple changed to bright orange, and the sun's orb disappeared over Henderson Peak, we headed down the trail, letting the twilight illuminate our way.

That night, Zamba didn't eat. I offered him all his favorite treats, but he just wasn't interested. The next morning, I noticed he had drunk quite a bit of water. I checked his temperature and found that he had a fever, and called the vet over to take a look.

"I can't see anything off the bat, but it's best to give him a complete checkup. Let me stop by a little later and we'll give him a more thorough exam."

By early afternoon, we were hard at work checking him out. I took his temperature again. It was still quite high. We gave him a shot of antibiotic, took a blood sample, and caught some urine for testing. We also gave him a shot of saline solution, to hydrate him and give him a little energy. The vet washed his hands and rolled down his sleeves.

"Let him rest awhile, and we'll check these out in the lab."

It took two days for the lab report to come back. His white blood count suggested that there was an infection somewhere in his body. I spoke to the vet.

"It's too dangerous to do an exploratory operation on him at his age. And there's always the possibility that we wouldn't find anything." He hesitated for a moment. "Ralph, it could just be old age."

"So what can we do?" I asked, not wanting to hear what he'd said.

"How old is he now?"

"Eighteen."

"That's pretty old for a lion, Ralph. In the wild, they're doing well if they see seven." He put his hand on my shoulder as I walked him to the door. "We'll take another look in the morning."

Zamba, a little bit wobbly, got up and moved to the sofa in the living room. It was quite large and comfortable, and his favorite place to watch television. When he was on it, there was little room for anyone else except little Tana, who came down to say good night.

"What's wrong with Zamba?" she asked.

"He's sick, honey."

I could see her confusion. Tana had always looked at Zamba as the protector of the other animals. How could he get sick? When she was very young, and afraid of the dark, I had sat on the edge of the bed and promised her that Zamba would watch over her as she slept, intercepting any nightmares. "Nothing can hurt you while he is watching, okay?"

She had worried about him getting enough sleep himself. "Don't worry, baby. He's Zamba, right?" She went to sleep, and never had a nightmare after that.

But now her protector was sick. We kissed good night, and she went to the couch, leaned over, and gave Zamba a good night kiss.

"Good night, brother. I'll see you later."

Zamba licked the back of her hand and tried to put his paw over her, but the effort was too much for him. He gave a low moan as he settled deep into the soft cushions.

After putting Tana to bed, Toni came downstairs. In many ways, she was more attuned to the ways of nature than I was. She gathered some blankets and covered Zamba, and we curled up and cuddled on a bit of sofa well into the night, quietly talking about Zamba's escapades and our lives together.

At about three o'clock in the morning, I noticed that Zamba was sweating, and seemed uncomfortable. He got up and moved into the kitchen, where he lay on the cool linoleum floor.

"Toni, you go on to bed now. I'll keep watch until morning."

She looked at me and understood that I wanted to be alone with him. I answered her thought.

"I'll be all right," I said.

We hugged each other, and I could feel her shaking with grief, an emotional tidal wave held just at bay.

"Don't worry," she said.

I kissed her good night and watched as she went upstairs. Even through my sadness, I knew how lucky I was.

I turned the kitchen light off, but left the oven door open so we had a bit of light. I got down on the floor with Zamba. He seemed more comfortable there, although his breathing was heavy and his body was soaked in sweat. He must have been chasing something in his dreams, because his legs moved most of the night.

I spread some extra blankets on the kitchen floor around him and put another one over him, and put my own body up against his to give him warmth. By four, his breathing had become more labored, and his pulse was faint and uneven.

I must have dozed off for a few minutes around five because I awoke at first light to find him looking at me. Dawn had broken pale and clear. His mane was soaked from sweat, and his ears lay wet against his head. He seemed exhausted, but those wonderful golden eyes looked at me with a steady gaze. We looked long at each other, saying all those things that cannot be said with words. I kissed his big nose. He licked where I had kissed him, and gave me a small lick on my face. He cuddled his great head into me, and together we drifted off into a peaceful sleep.

Early morning light shone through the window, and the house was quiet when I woke up. I reached out and touched Zamba's nose. It was cold and dry. His eyes were still open; he had never stopped looking at me. But God had left them.

I said his name and stroked his mane and rested my head on his silent chest. I buried my head into his mane and sobbed; I thought my own heart would break from the pain. At that moment, Toni came down and hugged me, and together we sat with him, with his massive head cradled in my lap. We sat and cried together, and told each other the stories of his many happy years.

When Tana came down we told her.

"Who's going to protect me tonight?" she cried.

"Zamba will always be there for you, baby."

Together Toni and I rolled Zamba onto a beautifully colored carpet and slid the carpet to the back door. I backed the station wagon up to the door, and with all our might we lifted him into the station wagon. We loaded the car with some tools and drove to the far end of the ranch, then up the hill to the Old Lady.

I pulled up as close as I could to the hidden entrance around the back. Opening the back hatch, we carefully slid Zamba's body down into the center clearing around the tree. Together we dug for hours down deep into the earth, careful not to disturb the roots. I sweated and cried as I dug, my stomach in a huge knot. The sun had come up, but the great Old Lady kept the heat away.

I looked over at Zamba's still body, tricking myself into thinking that he was just teasing, waiting for me to come over there so he could nuzzle me. But he was gone. I couldn't see for the tears as we dragged the blanket with him on it into the hole. It was deep; I didn't want him to ever be uncovered. I spread the blanket under him and smoothed it out. Then I put another on top of him, tucking him in as I had done so many times in bed.

"Well, old man—this is where we get off. I know you're not here, but be with my Snow Lion, and he'll take good care of you. Be part of the universe, my friend, and some day we'll meet again. You rest now, and I'll see you on the other side. I'll look forward to that."

I took off a medallion I had worn for years, an silver snake amulet with emerald eyes, and laid it on his neck. I stayed with him a moment, giving him a final hug and a kiss, and then filled the hole with fresh earth.

.   .   .

An enormous thunderstorm hit our ranch soon after Zamba died, and a bolt of lightning hit the Old Lady, splitting her in half. She had led a good life, and it was time for her to go. I like to think that she had been waiting for Zamba to show her the way.

 # TRIBUTE TO ZAMBA

It is with a humble presence that I write of a time past
when once there
lived a lion of great magnitude.
Born of a shared spirit between human and feline,
he existed in a world of
complex beings.
All who have had the privilege of knowing him felt his gift of love.
He possessed all of the true essence a lion can have—
His love of life, as well as the patience, understanding, and respect
that he
showed for
his human and animal family were his crowning achievements.
In his relationship with humans
He was the gentlest and most respected lion.
So, to my Lion,
ZAMBA
I offer a toast
To the happiness he so unselfishly gave

To his ability to see the good in others
And to see all things as positive.
You taught me well
I am so very proud to call you
My Lion
I will always love you,
ZAM

RDH

BOOKS BY RALPH HELFER

MODOC
The True Story of the Greatest Elephant that Ever Lived

ISBN 0-06-092951-0 (paperback)

Raised together in a small German circus town, a boy and an elephant formed a bond that would last their entire lives and would be tested time and again—through a near-fatal shipwreck in the Indian Ocean, an apprenticeship with the legendary Mahout elephant trainers in the Indian teak forests, and their eventual rise to circus stardom in 1940s New York City.

ZAMBA
The True Story of the Greatest Lion that Ever Lived

ISBN 0-06-076133-4 (paperback)

When a celebrated animal trainer takes a four-month-old African lion cub into his home, they care for each other, learn from each other, and change each other's lives, indelibly. With stories that range from the hilarious to the incredibly sad and poignant, *Zamba* will give any *Lion King* fan a new hero and touch every animal lover's heart. A one-of-a-kind love story.